BYE-BYE A

*Your 4 Steps To Greater Confidence,
Calmness and Contentment.*

Jonathan Butler

"This book succeeds in distilling a complex subject into a clear, practical and effective approach to making real change in your life. It brings the best of techniques such as NLP, CBT and hypnosis together to create a self-help program that really pushes the boundaries of how much can be taught in a book. The exercises are incredibly powerful and bring the secrets of therapy to a mass audience."

Andy Harrington, Sunday Times Best Selling Author - Passion Into Profit

"Jonathan worked with me using his mindset growth methodology to really help motivate me and take the action that I needed to succeed. His blend of deep experience, collaborative style and his understanding of how to apply the most incredible neuroscience in a business context was really powerful."

Tim Rawlinson, Elite Academy Manager Coach, the Premier League and Owner of Green Peak Consulting.

"I previously read the Chimp Paradox a few years ago and it reminds me of that book but with a more structured approach to fixing what is broken with the 21 Day time stamp. It really is very good."

Brent Jackson, Commercial Director, FloodFlash Insurance and Property Entrepreneur.

"Working with Jonathan and his amazing methods and tools has been truly game changing for me. I now appreciate just what I have achieved. I have renewed energy and belief in my actions. In just the last week I have been able to take in my stride a few operational issues that would previously have knocked me back"

Wendy Flanagan. Founder and Owner of the Holistic Home.

"I loved reading this. Practical, concise and with some great examples. It really resonated with me."

Nigel Field. Boardroom Advisor and former head of Transformation and people at Three.

"Jon is a very creative thinker who is able to simplify complex issues into tangible and practical solutions."

Dr Rick Norris. NHS Consultant Psychologist and Author of Think Yourself Fit.

"I think it is an excellent book and certainly made me think. I can think of many situations in my past that this know how would have been so helpful to have had."

Steve Howe, Rotary International, District Governor Elect, Great Britain and Ireland.

Bye-Bye Anxiety
Your Four Steps to Greater Confidence, Calmness and Contentment

This Simple but powerful 4 Step System uses scientifically proven principles[1] for delivering lasting change to your confidence, calmness and self-control in just 21 days.

In the light of the Covid-19 Pandemic this book can help anybody who has been knocked back by the changes to our lives. This book can help with overcoming anxiety, building self-confidence or getting back on track following life events such as divorce, loss or redundancy. These steps will enable you to think, feel and act differently in order to achieve lasting change in your life.

In our 'new normal' world there has never been a more important time to upgrade your mindset. In this world of constant change and greater uncertainty we need to reprogram ourselves to survive and thrive in this new environment. We cannot change everything that happens around us. We can however control better how we react and deal with life's challenges and opportunities.

Upgrading your thoughts and feelings will enable you to make dramatic and lasting change in your wellbeing, relationships and in achieving your life goals.

---

[1] *It's a very powerful means of changing the way we use our minds to control perception and our bodies.* Professor David Spiegel, Stanford University School of Medicine, 2016.

Enjoy the book and I really look forward to hearing your feedback.

Jonathan Butler.

Oxford, England, February 2021.

Table of Contents

Introduction 1

About the Author 3

Chapter 1: What You Need to Know About Your Mind 6

    You don't need to be an expert to understand your mind...........6

    Understand the Primary Functions of Your Mind 8

    Recognise the Power of Your Subconscious Mind 9

    Understand the Inputs to Your Mind. 11

    Word Associations that You Make 16

    What You Are Feeling Can be Changed 19

Chapter 2: Step 1 Recognise the Root Cause of Your Anxiety...22

    Nature. Am I Just Born this Way? 23

    Nurture. The Role of Your Parents 25

    Neuroscience. How Your Mind Tries to Help You 27

    Notice. What is Happening in Your Life Now? 29

    Exercise 1. What is your Root Cause Issue? The Root Cause Diagnostic Tool...31

    Exercise 2. Reflect on Your Learning 34

Chapter 3: Step 2 Reframe How You Think About Your Past ...36

    Exercise 3. Think About a Scenario of Your Own 41

Confront Your Past Events 42

Exercise 4 – Upgrade that Young You 42

Exercise 5. Upgrading Your Inner Child 46

Chapter 4: Step 3 Re-programme and Upgrade Your Thinking . 48

Purpose 49

Exercise 4. Build Yourself a Job or a Role Description 54

Exercise 5 - Write Down What You Want to Change 67

Exercise 6. See yourself in this better future 68

Exercise 7. Write Down Your Script 69

Need help? 71

Chapter 5: Step 4 Re-enforce Your New Habits and Beliefs 73

Creating Your Habit of Belief 76

Exercise 7. Audit Your Relationships 82

Exercise 8. Understand Others Communication Styles 84

Exercise 9. Reflect on Your Day 93

Further Help 94

Acknowledgements 95

Worksheets and hand-outs 97

The Script 98

Introduction

Maybe you are reading this book because you have been knocked sideways by recent world events. Perhaps you chose this book because you would just like to be more confident. Maybe you have always struggled with anxiety, but recent events have just brought everything to a head. Whatever the reason this book will show you the simple but powerful tools that can help you transform your levels of anxiety, self-belief and wellbeing. These techniques are powerful, safe and with a little work can deliver big improvements in your life in as little as 21 days.

Even before the outbreak of Covid-19 the world was facing a pandemic of mental health issues. In the US 18% of people suffer with chronic anxiety at any one time[2]. In the UK this figure is typically 17%[3]. During lockdown this figure grew to 62%.[4] Pre-Covid only around a third of people suffering sought help. Many of those third are prescribed medication or therapies such as Talking Therapy. The sad reality is that mental health services simply cannot cope with the demand. Doctors and General Practitioners have greater understanding than ever about mental

---

[2] Source Anxiety and Depression Association of America, 2020
[3] NHS England. (2016). Adult Psychiatric Morbidity Survey: Survey of Mental Health and Wellbeing, England
4 Mental Health Foundation, Coronavirus Mental Health Pandemic, March 2020

health, but they have too little time to help each patient. What's more the default option for anxiety type issues is simply to prescribe anti-depressants or other drugs. Big pharmaceutical companies still dominate the education, thinking and prescribing of the medical profession.

While these drugs can undoubtedly help people to cope, they are usually just dealing with the symptoms of anxiety, rather than addressing the root cause of why people have this anxiety

In this book I will show you that there is a different way and, I believe a better way. A way that does not require drugs, that deals with the root cause of anxiety and can deliver both rapid and lasting change.

In this book I will explain to you in simple and practical terms a powerful 4-step formula that could just change your life. This is a far better way than medication and a faster, more effective approach than the traditional Counseling or Talking Therapy approaches.

About the Author

Jonathan Butler is a renowned Therapist, Mindset Coach and Motivational Speaker. He has enabled hundreds of his individual clients to transform their confidence, massively reduce anxiety and resolve physical issues that are a direct result of anxiety. Britain's leading Therapist Marisa Peer personally trained him.[5]

Jonathan was an elite cyclist, winning Regional and National Titles in his native UK when he first came to understand the relationship between our mind and our body. He saw how performance could be significantly impacted by how we controlled our thoughts.

---

[5] Marisa Peer was named as Britain's best Therapist by Men's Health Magazine.

He took this knowledge into a highly successful career in the Tech Industry. Jonathan specialised in delivering ultra-high growth and turnaround agendas. Using his sport and business experience he developed a proven method to make rapid and lasting results to organisational performance. The bedrock of his transformation method was in creating greater personal and organisational belief.

In 2014 Jonathan became seriously ill after a business trip to Japan. The doctors were unable to diagnose what was wrong and he was off work for many months. He came to understand over time that his mind had been telling him that he was too stressed, pushing himself too hard and was sending a huge 'warning shot across his bows'. His mind was warning him that he needed to make major changes in his life.

In discovering the work of eminent experts such as Bruce Lipton, Carol Dweck and Marisa Peer he was able to build on his learned knowledge of how to turn around his own and other people's lives. Suffering from acute anxiety and depression Jonathan tried many types of Therapy alongside the usual prescribed medications. In desperation he turned to hypnotherapy and in particular Marisa Peer's more comprehensive Rapid Transformational Therapy (RTT) method to see if it could help him to properly move on. In the space of just a month this RTT treatment enabled him to understand where his anxiety came from, to be able to move on and to face up to dealing with all the challenges that he had been avoiding. It was truly life changing for Jonathan. Seeing so many other people in a similar situation to where he had been, Jonathan wanted to be able to share what he had learnt, to help others to rediscover their mojo.

As a result, Jonathan gave up the corporate world to help people who had lost their drive and purpose. He works as a Mindset Coach, Hypnotherapist and RTT Therapist with people who want to turn their lives around. He helps them change their subconscious thoughts and actions. He helps people from all walks of daily life. He has worked with Hollywood Actors, Elite Sportspeople and CEO's. Anxiety and depression do not discriminate by class, wealth or race. Even the most outwardly successful people often suffer with the most crippling anxiety.

Jonathan regularly talks at corporate events and has appeared on the BBC, Talk Radio New York and many regional media outlets. He works with clients in the UK, US, Europe, Middle East and Asia.

Chapter 1

What You Need to Know About Your Mind

You don't need to be an expert to understand your mind

When you understand your mind, you can control it and transform your feelings, thoughts, actions and results. In order to control your mind, you first need to understand some basic but very powerful concepts about your mind.

The brain is a very complex organ. Most books about the mind are very dry and frankly quite boring. I am fortunate enough to live near the beautiful city of Oxford in England. It is a place full of some of the world's greatest minds. I have been told by many academics here that the brain is so complex that we can never fully understand it. The brain may be very complex but what I have learned from those who have inspired me is that we can make it easy for anyone to understand what they need to know about their mind.

Master the key controls of your mind

Let me give you an analogy. The modern motor car is an incredibly complicated piece of technology. However, it is possible to be a skilled driver of that car without understanding the intricacies of the vehicle. You don't need to know how a combustion engine works to get the best from the car. You just need to understand the basic controls – the steering, the braking, the gear change and the instruments in the car. You can become an expert driver, even a racing driver without knowing too much about how it all works. You just need to understand the inputs that you give the vehicle to get the outputs that you want.

It is the same with your mind. There are just 4 areas that you need to master to drive your mind to get you the place that you want to go to. I will share this knowledge with you in this book.

First however it will help for you to understand some important and surprising points about your mind. This is stuff they will not have taught you in school and will really help make sense of why you think and act like you do.

Understand the Primary Functions of Your Mind

Our mind is designed to help us meet our most primal needs as human beings. It will put these needs above all others. This means its primary functions are to

1. Keep us alive
2. Keep us away from pain

For most of our evolution human beings have had to be alert to mortal dangers. We lived in a world where many things could kill us. In the Bronze Age 1 in 3 people died a brutal death. Our minds had to therefore be alert to these dangers to simply keep us alive. When we sense danger, we enter 'fight, flight or freeze' mode and pretty much shut down all non-essential functions.

To this day our minds are constantly alert to perceived dangers. We of course face far fewer mortal threats than our ancestors. We do however face far more 'triggers' for our fight, flight or freeze instincts. A wild animal may not eat us, but we may feel attacked by our boss or our colleagues. We may feel threatened by a customer. We may be attacked on social media. We may have events happen that remind us about our insecurities. In our modern, digital world the triggers of our insecurities are all constant and all pervasive.

These constant micro threats cause many of us to move from a useful level of anxiety, where we can focus on dealing with the threat and act effectively, to an overwhelming state of anxiety. When we feel constantly anxious it is debilitating. It makes you stressed and is likely to make you physically ill. I lose count of how many clients I have seen whose physical problems (asthma, eczema, IBS etc.) are simply results of chronic (consistent) anxiety in their lives.

Recognise the Power of Your Subconscious Mind

There are lots of parts to the Human Brain. Many with hard to remember and pronounce names. You do not need to know all of that! You just need to understand the concept that we have 2 minds. We have, a 'Conscious Mind' and a 'Subconscious Mind'. Your subconscious mind is the dominant force. Unlock your subconscious mind and huge change is possible in your life.

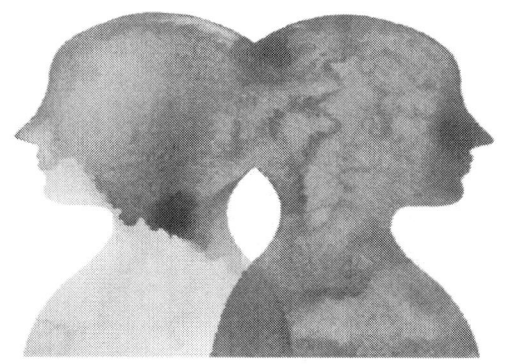

For true change you must change your subconscious thoughts.

Your conscious mind is the part of your mind where you make decisions in the moment. You are 'consciously' thinking about what you want to do in each situation. It is the rational part of your mind that assesses a situation and makes decisions based upon the facts that you have.

Your subconscious mind is like an autopilot function. It is the part of your brain that enables you to just do things without making conscious decisions. Imagine for example that you are driving your car. Unless you are new to driving you don't have to 'think' constantly about what to do. You subconsciously know how to steer, brake, change gear etc. If you make the same journey regularly you probably do this almost totally on autopilot. Have you ever driven somewhere and don't really remember anything about the journey? This is a classic example of your brain acting in the subconscious. Unless something unexpected happens on the journey, like a cat running out in front of you, there was no need to use your conscious mind at all.

What is vital to understand is that your subconscious is the most powerful part of your mind. Around 90% of everything that you do is controlled by your subconscious mind. This is the hard coding of your mind, or your mind's operating system. This hard coding mainly takes place during the first 7 years of your life. In this phase of your life your young brain is like a sponge, incredibly receptive to learning. We learn from the experiences we have and the environment around us.

This is clearly helpful. It means that everyday tasks like walking or talking do not require much thought. Imagine how overwhelming daily life would be if we had to think about these things? Our conscious mind only needs to kick in when we must make decisions. However, while the subconscious mind is a fantastic tool to allow us to do so many things without 'thinking' it does have some fundamental flaws in the modern world.

We live in a time of incredible change. This change, whether it is technological advances or societal change gets increasingly quicker. We as humans need to evolve and adapt to meet our ever-changing circumstances.

Why? Because if 90% of our actions come from our subconscious program and this program was largely coded when you were a child is it really fit for purpose for you today? Does it help you or hinder you as an adult, needing to adapt to this fast-changing world?

Your mind is a very powerful computer. Your subconscious is your Operating System, and you are still running an operating system that was written when you were a young child. Would you buy a new laptop with a 20,30 or 40-year-old operating system? So why do you allow your mind to work with this out-dated code?

Understand the Inputs to Your Mind.
Images as Commands.

Your mind is a computer. Instead of having a keyboard however your mind has its own 'input' devices. The primary input 'commands' that your mind responds to are the images that you give it and the words that you use.

Images are very powerful. You have probably heard the expression that a picture speaks a thousand words. Well, there is a lot of merit in that expression. If you have ever had to sit through a boring presentation with someone presenting lots of PowerPoint slides you will know what I mean. People write masses of detail on slides. The reality is it's overwhelming and the audience just switch off. A presentation with far less words and a few powerful visuals is however far more effective.

Tell your mind where you want to go

Let me explain something important about how your mind works. You already know that your subconscious mind is the dominant part of your mind. Your subconscious beliefs and thoughts are always guiding your decision- making. When you are faced with a new situation your mind goes back into its memory to decide how it feels about what is happening. If you are over a certain age think of it like your mind has a hard drive full of memories. Think of it as 'machine learning' where your mind is making decisions based upon your past choices or preferences.

Let me give you a simple example. When I was at my primary school, they used to serve the most disgusting rice pudding. It was grey, it was watery, and it was usually luke-warm. Are you getting the picture? What's worse they used to put a coin in the cooking pot to encourage us to eat the rice pudding in case we found the coin. If that didn't work, we were not allowed to leave the table until we ate it all up!

Unsurprisingly I grew up to hate rice pudding. Every time I heard the words rice pudding, I saw this image of grey, watery and luke-warm gruel. I also associated it with images of losing my playtime. Once I was 'lucky' enough to get the 10 pence coin. Fortunately, I did not choke on it but now the thought of rice pudding made it hard for me to swallow. For years swallowing any kind of a tablet gave me a mental block. It was all because of the time the 5-year-old me put as spoonful of rice in my mouth and almost choked on that ten pence piece. Our mind really is smart!

Words as Commands

"Sticks and Stones may break my bones but calling names won't hurt me." So many of these familiar phrases are grounded in reality. This one however is absolute nonsense. It's a phrase that has been used to excuse bad behaviour and bullying for too long. Actually, bones heal quickly, especially for children. They repair themselves perfectly. As you learned earlier in this Chapter about the primary functions of our mind, constant hurtful words, especially from parents, teachers or groups of other children can cause serious or lasting damage. In my private practice I see people in their 50's and 60's who are still damaged from the words that they heard as a child.

Words are mightier than the sword

I am not talking about the occasional nasty or thoughtless word. I am not in favour of turning our children into snowflakes. The world can be a harsh place and children need to build resilience. However, repeated inappropriate words and behaviours over a sustained period will affect even the strongest of people. If any child is constantly told they are worthless they will come to believe that deep in their subconscious.

There is then the matter of the words that we give ourselves. These can be just as damaging as the words of significant others. If we hear negative words from others, we can perpetuate the beliefs and thoughts that we have about ourselves. We can't always control the words of others. As I will talk about further in this book, we can however limit our exposure to the words of others. We can fully control our own words and I cover this in detail later.

Since we began to communicate the great, the good and the not so good have realised the power of words to influence others. Words are evocative. Skillful orators can use words to significant effect. Think about Winston Churchill and his "we shall fight them on the beaches speech". These carefully crafted words were able to lift a nation on the verge of capitulation to raise spirits and continue what seemed like a lost cause in holding out against the seemingly unstoppable Nazi Germany. Think about Martin Luther King and his famous "I have a dream" speech. A speech so powerful and moving that it was pivotal in advancing the pace of change for civil rights in the USA.

On the flip side the bad people have also learned how to use words to frighten people, to mobilise people against an imagined enemy and to commit atrocities in the name of a country or cause. Adolf Hitler was able to use words (and pictures) to turn the people of one of the world's most educated and cultured nations into delivering the Holocaust, just a generation ago.

You as an individual have the same choices. You can choose to use the power of words for good or for bad in your own life. You can inspire or depress yourself. You can inspire or inhibit those around you. The words you use are commands to your mind. They are like keyboard stokes that you input into the software of your computer and if constantly repeated can create a deep belief in your subconscious. Your mind doesn't judge whether the command is right. It simply follows your command without question.

So, are you going to inspire and empower yourself or are you going to depress and inhibit yourself? It is your choice. You are an adult now. You can't control your past, but you can take responsibility for your future.

Repetition creates habits

Your mind does not make value judgments. It just tries to give you what it thinks that you want. So, if you have a habit of telling yourself negative thoughts, your mind will believe this and make you into someone who lacks belief and always thinks the worst. If you constantly give yourself positive words your mind will see the world through a different lens. You will be more open to opportunity and less afraid of failure.

Word Associations that You Make

If you have ever played a game of 'word associations', you will know that words can trigger very personal associations. For me if someone says, "rice pudding" I might say "grey" or "disgusting." Here are associations that I regularly see with my clients

Food Associations

People who are struggling with weight often have a problematic relationship with food. If you grew up in a household where food was a source of comfort food is likely to become an issue. Maybe your parents gave you sweets or cake when you were sad. Perhaps when they were not able to give you the time you wanted, they let you eat what you wanted. Possibly your mother turned to chocolate when she was stressed, and you developed this same habit.

Food is often a substitute for affection, love or human comfort. When we do not have access to those basic human needs, we look for whatever source of comfort is available to us.

Alcohol Associations

What does alcohol mean to you? What did you observe at an early age? What alcohol habits have you developed?

Especially in Northern Europe, alcohol has become synonymous with relaxing. Maybe you get home from work and you have a drink 'to relax'. Drinking has become almost essential to socialise or to talk to the opposite sex Perhaps Friday nights were about letting your hair down and of course drinking. Holidays were time to drink more. Watching the football or watching a movie often involves a beer or a glass of wine. We celebrate special occasions with a drink. We drown our sorrows with a drink. We calm our nerves with a drink. This behaviour is so ingrained in our culture.

You will have pictures of alcohol in that hard drive in your subconscious mind to support all those scenarios. You will have learned this, and it has become a deeply embedded habit. If for example you turn to drink when you have had a bad day this is because when you feel sad your brain is pulling up the video that says, 'when you are sad you need a drink to escape from reality.'

Relationship Patterns

Everyone wants to have a good relationship. To be loved, to be valued, to feel safe. Why then do so many people stay in bad relationships that give them none of these things? Why also do some people continue to recreate the pattern of moving from one bad relationship to another?

Typically, people who have these kind of relationship problems have grown up around unhealthy relationships. They may want something better, but these types of relationships become familiar too them. Were your parents abusive to each other? Even though it made you unhappy your subconscious mind is likely to be drawn to similar relationships. These relationships are familiar and normal to your mind. You can also believe that anything better is simply not available to you.

Work Associations

Have you ever noticed how confident people who are confident talking 121 are terrified of speaking in public? Have you ever had a colleague who never stops talking but in meetings never says a word? Doesn't that seem strange?

I had a client who was an extremely well-known Academic. He was an expert in his subject and his speaking events would sell out almost instantly. One to one he was very engaging and very charming. However, the idea of standing in front of his students terrified him. He would have panic attacks. Despite all his success, subconsciously, he didn't believe he was good enough and was terrified that people would laugh at him. It made no logical sense to him.

He came to me to ask for help. He wanted to stop feeling this way. It was making him ill. He had to stand in front of audiences every day for his work. He could not cope with this level of anxiety daily.

We discovered in our appointment that he had been Dyspraxic as a child. Under hypnosis with me he recalled subconscious memories as a child in school. He recalled the other children laughing at him when he couldn't read a word correctly. He also recalled overhearing his teacher tell his parents that he would never be able to succeed in anything academic.

So, what was happening now was that every time he had to present in front of an audience his mind was subconsciously drawing upon those 2 memories. Remember that the mind always wants to keep us away from pain? Every time he had to stand up and talk to an audience his subconscious was warning him that this was a painful thing to do – where everyone would laugh at you. This second memory was his subconscious reminding him not to get ahead of himself. How can you feel confident talking to Oxford Undergraduates when you have a deep-rooted subconscious belief set by your Primary School Teacher that you will never amount to anything?

What You Are Feeling Can be Changed

Fortunately, you can learn to change the pictures that have been guiding you. I now love rice pudding. I have been able to erase that picture. My brilliant Professor client has replaced his childhood picture of being laughed at with a picture of the brightest students from across the world hanging on his every word.

Just as we can take on these unhelpful and limiting pictures, we can also take on helpful and enabling pictures. I will explain how later in the book

If you are suffering from anxiety or stress don't be too hard on yourself. You are just responding to nature and to the triggers around you. It is not your fault. Because of the real threats that humans faced in the past we are hard wired to feel this way. One of the things we do is go to what is called an Automatic Negative Though (or an ANT) when we feel triggered by an external event. This is a protection mechanism that we carry around from a time when safety was our primary concern, when we lived in a time that there was clear mortal danger.

The problem today is that we are still saddled with these ANT's. We do need this protection mechanism, but we need to upgrade our assessment of situations based upon the situation that we find ourselves in today

You can take charge of your own future.

The good news is that you can take control of your anxiety. You can upgrade that operating system that you were given as a child.

Even better news is this. You can change your reaction to triggers. It is not hard to upgrade your thoughts. It does not involve years of therapy. It does not take a lot of hard work and what you need to do is simple.

There are just 4 steps that you need to follow to make this change. This is change that can be realised in as little as 21 days and when the process is followed provides lasting results. This process is based on the latest understanding of neuroscience, proven therapy techniques, involves no harmful drugs and could change your life. In the following Chapters I explain the 4 simple steps that you can take to get you from where you are now to where you want to be.

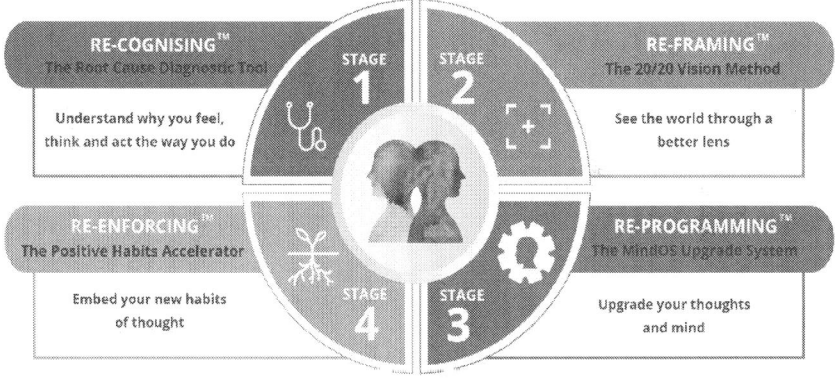

Chapter 2

Step 1
Recognise the Root Cause of Your Anxiety

Much of our healthcare services are focused upon dealing with the presenting symptoms. The lack of resources, the time constraints of GP's and the power of the pharmaceutical companies all contribute towards the emphasis on treating the symptoms rather than getting to the root cause of anxiety related issues.

To properly overcome anxiety related conditions, we really need to understand why we are anxious in the first place. If we fail to do this any treatment is just applying a sticking plaster to the problem. What is required to address this (and any engineering problem) is a Root Cause Analysis. Only when we understand the root cause can we give the correct solution. If your car keeps overheating you need to do more than just keep filling it up with more water. We need to understand where the fault is deep in the cooling system. When we understand this we can make the correct fix and have belief that the car will function as it should. It is the same for our mind.

To understand where our anxiety comes from in the first place, we need to look at four areas. The Four N's of

1. **N**ature
2. **N**urture
3. **N**euroscience
4. **N**otice

 Nature. Am I Just Born this Way?

Academics like to debate whether nature or nurture has the greatest impact upon how people develop. We are clearly the product of the genes that we inherit from our parents. We certainly inherit physical characteristics. Medical conditions too can run in families.

Consider however how differently brothers and sisters can be. I am sure you know families where the characters, the interests, the intelligence and the motivations of the children can be very different. The reality is that while we share genes and characteristics, we are all very individual.

How you feel is not set for life

I often hear from clients that a condition they have 'runs in the family.' It may be true that their condition is genetic. However, when children hear from an early age that having a condition runs in the family, they will also believe that this condition is inevitable for them. It can become a self-fulfilling prophecy.

This applies not just to physical conditions but to skills or abilities too. I know that in my own family we were told that 'no one is any good at maths in our family'. Guess what? My sister and I always had a mental block with maths. We believed we were no good at it and always became anxious about any task involving maths.

I believe that of course our genes have a role in how we develop. However, I believe that most of us are born perfect, both physically and mentally. We are not born believing that "I am no good at maths" or "depression is a family trait." We come to believe these things and make them our reality. When we believe we are no good at maths we start to believe that it's hard, we get anxious at the idea of maths lessons and we avoid the subject wherever possible. Of course, then we are no good at maths. We have made ourselves believe this.

So, whether we are truly born this way or not, we do not need to be defined by being or believing we were 'born this way'. We have the power to change the way we think. Changing how we think changes how we feel. When we change how we feel we can change how we act. When we change how we act we change the outcomes that we get.

 Nurture. The Role of Your Parents

Remember in Chapter 2.2 we talked about the role of the Subconscious mind? Remember how the subconscious mind controls most of what we do? Remember also that the sub-conscious thoughts you have, developed very early in your life? So, most of the things that you subconsciously believe were coded into your operating system as a child.

When we are young children, we are incredibly receptive to learning. Our mind is in a highly receptive Theta Brain State. It is like a sponge, soaking up everything it sees and hears. As we pass the age of 8 years old these experiences form our hard coded beliefs about ourselves and the world in which we live.

The main source of our information and beliefs as children comes from the significant people around us. This is usually our parents. We also however take on board beliefs about the world we live in and, critically, about ourselves from teachers, coaches, older siblings, grandparents, priests or others who have a significant presence or role in our young lives.

Nurture determines growth

Have you ever found yourself saying "I am turning into my mother/ father?' Most of us do as we get into our 40's and beyond. It is because we form our beliefs and behaviours from our parents at a young age and even many years later still copy their values and behaviours. We may not actually display these behaviours until much later in life. So when we become parents, we naturally end up saying and doing the same things as our parents did with us.

Of course, we take on many good things from the nurture of our parents. It is powerful learning by example. However, we can also inherit unhelpful and even deeply damaging thoughts, feelings and habits from our parents.

A highly anxious mother is likely to have children who grow up being anxious and worrying about everything. This is because the children will take on board the beliefs, words, behaviours and habits of the mother. If the person who looks after you most and who you look to for all your basic needs makes you believe that there is danger everywhere you will likely grow up feeling this way. Unless you interrupt that cycle you will likely pass on this same affliction to your own children.

Parents in poor households, living in a poor part of town can similarly pass on their money worries and struggles to their children. Children growing up in underprivileged environments will often believe and perpetuate what they see and hear from their parents. "We can't afford that". "Money doesn't grow on trees." We could never have that." All of these are beliefs that children will take on board.

Conversely if you are a child born into a situation of privilege you have very different beliefs. You see opportunity, money and choices. Boris Johnson probably felt from a very young age that he could be Prime Minister. In his family, in his school, in his social circle this was eminently achievable from the examples and expectations he would have grown up with. The beliefs that a child develops about their potential on the playing fields of Eton are very different to the child growing up in inner City Baltimore, Philadelphia or Middleborough.

 Neuroscience. How Your Mind Tries to Help You

Our mind may be complicated, but its key functions are very simple. I covered earlier in this Chapter how your mind is hard coded to meet your most basic needs. It wants to keep you safe and it wants to stop you being hurt (emotionally as well as physically). It also wants to make you happy.

There is so much going on in our heads

Now here is where it gets really interesting! Your mind has learned from evolution to recognise danger and develop a fight, flight or freeze instinct when it senses danger or threat. However, your mind also develops a library of memories from your early life that it draws upon to determine how it should respond to a situation in your life now. This is like a library or a hard drive of videos that your mind draws upon in each situation. So, when you encounter a situation now your mind will go back into the library and ask "how should I react?"

Let me give you an example from a client of mine. Let's call her Jane. When Jane was 5, she was chased and bitten by a dog. Ever since then she has been terrified of dogs. The mere sight of a dog, no matter how small or cute makes her panic. She gets short of breath, she feels anxious and tense in her stomach, she sometimes gets a cold sweat. This is because when she sees a dog, her mind goes back to the video of that event and tells Jane that dogs are dangerous, and she runs away. Her mind is trying to protect her from danger. It thinks it is helping her.

While this is totally logical it clearly is unhelpful to spend your life fearing dogs. For many people with this same experience, they would spend their whole life fearing dogs. I was able to help Jane to realise that she no longer needed to be controlled by her 5-year-old mind and change her autopilot function to be the adult woman that she now was. And have no fear of dogs. I will explain in the next Chapter just how we reframe' her view of that experience.

 ## Notice. What is Happening in Your Life Now?

Maybe you are suffering right now with anxiety. Remember that a little bit of anxiety is normal and is helpful. When that anxiety is constant or overwhelming however it causes major issues in your life. Unchecked, this kind of constant anxiety will affect your mental well-being and quite probably your physical wellbeing. To deal with this anxiety you really need to get to the root cause. Only when you can identify the root cause of your chronic or disproportionate acute anxiety can apply the right 'fix' to your problem.

Look carefully at what is happening

Have you ever taken your car to the garage with a problem and they say they don't really know what the cause is? They then say we will start with changing this part and see if that works? How frustrating is that? How time consuming and costly is that? Often you can spend a whole bunch of money and much of your precious time only for the problem to still be there!

For many people it is the same with Therapy. Week after week, month after month of Talking Therapy that costs a lot of money and sucks up your valuable time. We need a better way that immediately gets to the root cause and deals with the real underlying issue. What I have learnt is that you can identify the root cause of your issues and quickly and effectively deliver the right Therapy. In my individual sessions with my clients, I use a technique called regression, that I was taught by Marisa Peer, to help them identify how, when, where and why they developed the belief that they needed to be anxious (or whatever their issue is).

I can't do regression with each of you who is reading this book. However, I have used my knowledge to develop a tool that will allow you to understand the likely causes of your issue. I call this the Root Cause Diagnostic Tool ™

In my experience most people's root cause of anxiety, depression or loss of confidence is a result of one or more of what I call the LOWS in early life. LOWS are events that made us feel that

We are **not**	**LOVABLE**
We do **not have**	**OPPORTUNITIES**
We are simply **not**	**WORTHY**
We **do not feel**	**SAFE**

Exercise 1. What is your Root Cause Issue? The Root Cause Diagnostic Tool

Circle or highlight any issue that applies to you in your life right now from the following rows. Circle as many as apply

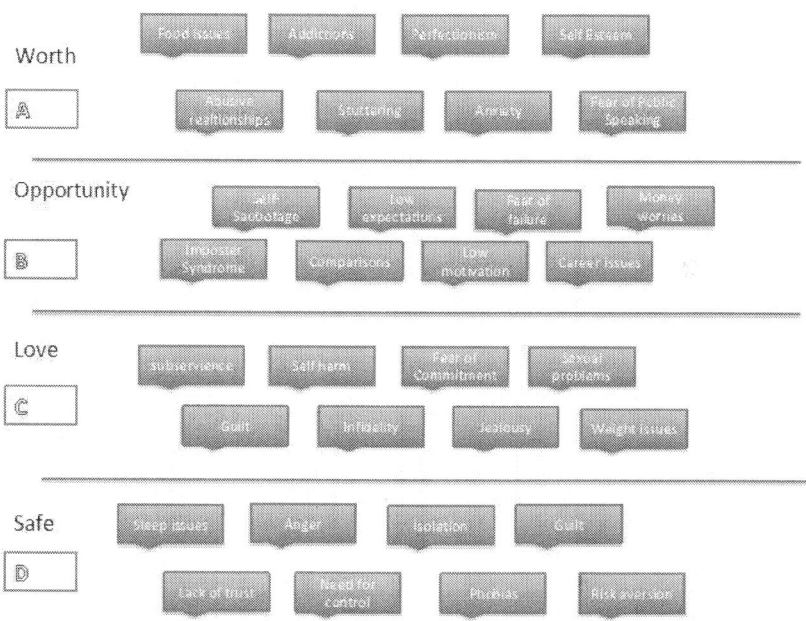

Interpreting Your Results

Ok Sherlock what does this mean?

If you circled **mostly A's** you have deep rooted issues about being Lovable. Maybe your parents separated or divorced when you were young. Perhaps you never felt you got attention from your parents. Maybe your parents told you that you were a 'mistake.' Possibly you lived in a house where there was little affection or physical contact. Maybe you were rarely told that you were loved. Possibly you were the youngest of many children or maybe you were adopted. All these types of 'nurture' childhood scenarios can contribute to insecurities and feelings that you are not truly lovable.

If you circled **mostly B's** this indicates that you have deep seated issues about the opportunities that you believe are available (or more importantly not available) to you. Maybe you grew up in a house where money was tight. Maybe you were used to hearing comments such as 'That's not for people like us". Perhaps you grew up in an area and went to school with low aspirations. Maybe your parents were unemployed, or you regularly heard that there was no money left by the end of the week. When we grow up in this kind of environment our young mind will easily believe that its opportunities are limited. It's easy to believe that you will never amount to anything. Your mind doesn't want you to be hurt or disappointed with life, so it tries to protect you by setting your bar of expectation very low

If you circled **mostly C's** this usually indicates that you have issues with your Self Worth. This is usually a result of childhood experiences that made you feel you were never good enough. Maybe you had parents who you could never please. Perhaps your parents were high achievers or perfectionists. Perhaps you had a teacher who criticised your work or told you that you would never amount to anything. Maybe you had siblings who always made you feel that you were just not as worthy as them. Perhaps you were bullied at school because you were different.

If you circled **mostly D's** you likely had a lot of childhood worries over safety and security. I find this is very common with people who have grown up in households where they saw violence or felt the threat of violence. This could also apply to people who were bullied or abused at boarding schools or in Children's Homes. Children who have grown up in countries with conflict also feel this constant threat. If you have suffered with PTSD as an adult rather than having childhood issues this would also apply. This could encompass military experiences, violence or abusive relationships.

If you circled a **lot of A's and a lot of C's.** This reflects that a lack of perceived love as a child often permeates into feelings of lack of worth. For instance, children whose that' divorce often feel that somehow, they must not have been worth staying around for. As we shall cover later this is patently not the case, but it is natural for our young selves to take on board these feelings about ourselves.

Exercise 2. Reflect on Your Learning

Before moving on to the next Chapter spend some time to reflect upon what you have read and learnt in this Chapter. Take some space and some quiet time to think about what you have learnt. Give yourself at least 2 sitting of 30 minutes to really think about events in your memory that relate to your 'root cause issue.

Think deeply about what events come to mind? When do you first remember feeling this way in your life? Think of them like scenes in a film. Write these memories or scenes down.

You will find that scenes will come back to you and you will likely get some 'light bulb moments' where you can understand how certain events made you take on beliefs about yourself.

When you have written down these events that you think are significant look over these written words as if you are a detective looking for pieces of evidence. What is this evidence from your past indicating about how you feel right now?

For example, if you are drawn back to scenes of being laughed at in school when you spoke in front of the class and today you get panic attacks if you must talk to a large group you have a compelling piece of evidence.

Remember that how you think about yourself will influence how you feel. How you feel will influence how you act. In turn how you act will influence the results and outcomes you get in your life. Much of what we think about ourselves as an adult is still based upon these beliefs that we took on board as children.

These past events no longer need to define you. You can upgrade your beliefs to reflect the situation that you are in today and how you want to think, feel and act in the future. In the next Chapter I explain how you can do this.

Chapter 3

Step 2
Reframe How You Think About Your Past

RE-FRAMING™
The 20/20 Vision Method

To see these past events differently we need to 'Reframe' how we see them. This literally means looking at these events through a different lens or filter. Right now, you are looking at that issue based upon a different time, place and situation that occurred as a child. You need to look at it through the lens that you need and is available to you today.

There are 3 'C Steps' that we need to address to deliver a 'reframe'

1. **Challenge** the views that you have relied upon
2. **Confront** how you see your past events
3. **Contextualise** the situation that you are in today

So now you should understand how you take on board beliefs

about yourself based upon a combination of your Nature (what we are born with) and our Nurture (the experiences of your childhood). Your interpretation of these events leads to your LOWS (Not Lovable, lack Opportunity, lack Worth or lack Safety).

It is important to understand is that it is often not the severity of the events that we may have experienced as a child but rather the importance that we place upon them. I see clients who have had extremely difficult childhoods, suffering from significant trauma or abuse. It is easy for a Therapist or a Counsellor to jump to the conclusion that this is the root cause of the presenting issue. Sometimes however the event that started the feelings, when looked back upon today, seems quite trivial. In my individual client work, as an RTT Therapist, I regress people under hypnosis to rapidly understand what events really caused the issue rather than jumping to a wrong conclusion.

In my work as a Therapist, I have had many ex-military people seek help from me. In a case that I remember well, based on our 'Discovery' discussion it would have been easy to jump to the conclusion that the issue was Post Traumatic Stress. The trauma they suffered in the military was the trigger to release feelings about themselves. The root cause of their issue however was from childhood events. The military training was able to prepare him for the things he witnessed in service in Iraq. Where he was really struggling was related to how his schoolteacher made him feel.

Remember Jane from Chapter 3? Jane was terrified of dogs because a dog bit her when she was 5. To overcome this fear as an adult she needed to reframe this experience. She was still seeing this memory through the frame of a 5-year-old girl. She needed to start seeing this event through the frame of a grown woman with children of her own. When she was able to do this reframing, she could really start to change her reactions to how she saw and felt about dogs.

She was able to realise that the dog only bit her because she kept pulling its tail. She could start to see this 5-year-old child provoking a dog, scaring a dog until eventually the dog literally snapped. She was able to see that she was no longer a 5-year-old. She could see that there was no way now that she would do that to the dog. She could also see that the dog only gave her a tiny nip. It scared her but it didn't really hurt. She could see that the dog was scared and that it had no history of biting people. She was able to laugh about the event that she had been so scared about for all of those years.

Her subconscious mind however had taken on board the belief at 5 years old that dogs were dangerous. Understandably so. Through reframing that memory, by looking at it through the frame of a grown woman she was able to see that there was no reason to fear dogs anymore. What's more she was determined not to pass this fear onto her own daughter. Doing a reframe helped her to think far more rationally about her reactions to dogs.

So, let me explain the process for making this change

The 20/20 Vision Method

To reframe how we see these past events we need to look through a different lens or frame. This is done through the three steps of my 20/20 Vision Method.

 **Challenge Your Thoughts**

Remember the ANT's? Those pesky 'Automatic Negative Thoughts? Remember that it is natural to think that way because your mind's primary purpose is to try and protect you. So that little girl's mind thought that dogs were a danger to her and made sure that she would stay away from dogs in future with ANT's about all dogs.

While it may be understandable to feel that way, it is far from helpful to feel that way. So here is what you must do to look at things in a more balanced or positive frame. Firstly, you need to challenge the veracity of that thought.

When you have a negative thought about a situation you need to firstly stop and question that thought before you react to it. Is that thought right? Are there other possible explanations or scenarios for what is happening.? Let me give you an example

Sue is walking down the street towards the shops. She sees Sarah, one of the other mums from school coming the other way on the opposite side of the street. She doesn't know Sarah well but had a good chat with her outside the school gates just a week ago. She had decided that she would invite her round for a coffee the next time that she saw her. Sue starts to wave at Sarah, but Sarah just carries on walking past and doesn't respond at all.

Sue feels crestfallen. "Why did she ignore me?" She feels humiliated that she was waving at this woman in public, only to be ignored. She then starts a whole cycle of Automatic Negative Thoughts such as 'this woman doesn't like me', 'I must be boring' and nobody likes me.

The next day she sees Sarah again at the school gates and now she is feeling angry. 'Who the hell does this woman think she is?'. She makes a point of not looking at Sarah. 'If she is going to ignore me, I will ignore her'

Later that week Sue has a coffee with one of her friends and tells her about the experience. Her friend laughs and says "oh Sarah has her head in the clouds all the time. She wouldn't notice if a two tonne Gorilla stepped out in front of her."

Sue feels bad now. She realises she was wrong. She got herself all worked up about nothing and then made a very deliberate point of ignoring Sarah at the school gates. All of this happened because she didn't challenge the thought and jumped to an Automatic Negative Thought about what happened. Here is what she could have done.

Sue could have thought about alternative reasons as to why Sarah did not respond to her wave. Here are my possible alternatives. See if you can think of more

1. Sarah was short sighted and did not see her.
2. Sarah was having a bad day and her thoughts were somewhere else.
3. Sarah did not recognise her.
4. Sarah was talking to somebody else on the phone.
5. Sarah is very shy.
6. What I would have suggested to Sue after this experience would be to sit and write these alternative scenarios down. Just by writing these down it makes the possible alternative explanations more real. Most importantly however it will make Sue feel much better. It will help her to avoid going to that ANT and the whole series of negative thoughts, emotions and actions that follow.

Exercise 3. Think About a Scenario of Your Own

Think of a scenario that happened to you. Think of a time recently where somebody really annoyed or upset you. Think of how you felt. What were the thoughts that you were having? How did you your body feel? Just home in on those sensations that you experienced.

What was the ANT that you jumped to? How did it make you feel? What were the alternative scenarios to that ANT. Write down all these scenarios. Look at them. Now think about the alternative thoughts of each scenario.

Now think about that situation again. How could you have reacted differently? Would it have been better had you considered these alternative scenarios?

Make sure that you

- Challenge the original thought
- Compare different alternative explanations
- Clarify how you think about the original thought now

Now picture yourself in that same scenario again, having considered alternatives to your ANT. See what you see. Hear what you hear. Most importantly feel what you feel. Really focus in on the feeling having reframed your potential view of what happened. Notice the change in physical sensations when you consider other, less negative alternative explanations to how you originally viewed the event

 **Confront Your Past Events**

Find a quiet space where you can sit and reflect on what you learned in Section 2 about the root cause of your issues. There are four key LOWS root causes. Not believing that you are Lovable, that you lack Opportunity, that you lack Worth or that you do not feel safe

Now we are going to help you to see these root cause events in a different way. Sit somewhere where you will not be disturbed and where you can really focus.

Exercise 4 – Upgrade that Young You

Marisa Peer uses a wonderful tool called Upgrading the Child. In my work as an RTT Therapist this is often one of the most powerful moments of transformation that I see with clients.

Picture yourself as that young child who has taken on board these subconscious beliefs. See yourself sitting in your bedroom, upon your bed. Just observe that young you for a few moments. How is he or she feeling? See what they are seeing in that bedroom. Just feel yourself going right back to that place that was so familiar to you. See what you saw, hear what you heard and most importantly just feel what you felt.

If you are getting good memories and feelings, that is great! You can just let those good feelings wash over you. If you get good memories, you can skip the rest of this exercise.

If that young child is feeling sad, unhappy or in some other way feeling bad about themself, I want you to visualise yourself as you are now going back into that bedroom. Sit down on the bed with them and wrap your arms around. Make that young you feel secure, loved and understood.

I want you to then bring that young you back to your life now. Imagine that you are putting them in your car and bringing them back into your life now. As a child you had a limited voice and you had limited choices. Now as an adult you are free to make your own choices, to choose the company you keep and to make your own decisions. You also have your own voice. You have a right to be listened to.

Now close your eyes and think about what that young you needed to hear to feel better about themselves. What they needed to hear will obviously be specific to that young you and your situation. It will also vary according to which of the 3 LOWS root causes are relevant to you.

- You didn't feel loved (L)
- You didn't believe opportunities were available to you (O)
- You didn't feel worthy (W)
- You didn't feel safe (S)

Now select 4 or 5 phrases from this chart that really resonate for you. Feel free to tweak the wording to suit you and how you would express the same sentiment. Maybe you have phrases of your own that work better for you. Whether you use these phrases or your own, write them down. No more than 4 or 5.

What did you need to hear?

Now close your eyes, visualise yourself holding that young you and tell him or her what they needed to hear. If you can, say it out loud. Keep repeating it over and over. Picture that young you, hearing these words. Notice the change in them and in you. You may feel yourself becoming lighter, happier and more relaxed. Maybe you feel like a weight is being lifted. Picture a big warm, soft blanket wrapping around you both. Do this for around 5 minutes. Then spend another 5 minutes just taking in the sensation.

ACTION

Repeat the final part of this exercise (from the previous paragraph) every day for the next week. If possible, do this just before you go to bed to make it your daily ritual. If you said prayers before bed as a child, think of it like this, making it your 'salvation of yourself' time. If you are a commuter, you can also do this in the train or on public transport as you travel. Whatever works for you. Just do this as many times in a day as you can. Consistency and repetition are key.

This process of bringing the young you into your world is incredibly powerful. It forms an important bridge for helping take that young you away from insecurity or lack of power that you had to a feeling of greater security and worth.

 **Contextualise Your Situation**

Having challenged your thoughts in Exercise 4, you will have really begun to embed this feeling by repeating this exercise every day.

The context of your life now is likely very different to the context in which you first took on board these limiting beliefs about yourself. The next step in the process of reframing how you think about your events is to make clear to your mind that you are now in a totally different situation.

If you took those unhelpful thoughts on board as a child, you are living in a different scenario right now. When you are a child you have limited power. You have a limited voice. You have limited choices. You have limited physical strength. You cannot choose where you live or who you live with.

As an adult you are in a very different position. Even if you feel that your life is not great you do have significantly more choice and a greater voice than you had as a child. You do not have to live in a certain place. You can choose who you live with and you can make many choices about yourself.

You may have feelings of being trapped. You may feel that you are trapped in a job, a relationship or some other situation. Unless you are in prison however you are not trapped or limited in the same way as that young you was. You are trapped in your thinking, creating your own boundaries and constraints.

If your issues did not come about in childhood but came about later in life as a result of trauma your situation is slightly different. However, you are most likely still in a different situation. If you are a veteran suffering with PTSD you are not likely to still be in the front line where the trauma occurred. The trauma that you experienced however is keeping your mind on high alert to any trigger of being in that same situation

Exercise 5. Upgrading Your Inner Child

There are many variants of reparenting you inner child, as originally developed by Lucia Capacchione in 1976.[6] This is used extensively to great effect by RTT Therapists. Here is a powerful exercise based upon the Inner Child technique that you can use.

Picture that young you again looking back on the place that they were in. Feeling what they felt, hearing what they heard. Now fill in the gaps in the affirmation statements below. Put in whatever words come to mind and are powerful for you

1. I am not that child anymore because I have a voice now
2. I am not that child anymore because I choose my company now
3. I am also not that child because (……………………)
4. I long since stopped being that child
5. I am an adult now

---

[6]

6. I will never be that child again because (..................)

Now I want you to say these 6 statements out loud. Say it as many times as you want. Feel yourself letting go. You are not that child. You have a voice; you have a choice. You are responsible for your own better future.

If your root cause was trauma as an adult, then simply change the words above to reflect this.

Now add these affirmations to your daily ritual in the previous exercise and say every day.

Change your frame and change your life

Chapter 4

Step 3
Re-programme and Upgrade Your Thinking

This is the Step that that I really love. This is where you learn to re-programme your mind. This is where you learn to have better, more empowering and more helpful thoughts. Remember that helpful thoughts lead to better actions and of course better outcomes. This approach is based upon the principles of Neuroplasticity, the recognition that our minds can develop new pathways and connections. Much of the techniques that are still used in mainstream therapies are based upon the works of Freud and Jung. While there has been some evolution many therapists are working with tools based upon work from the early 20th Century! Much of these resulting talking therapies work with helping people to understand where their issues come from. Neuroplasticity represents the latest thinking in neuroscience and allows focus on literally changing how you think. After all, it may be interesting to understand where issues come from but what people really want is move forward and get results.

Your mind is just like a computer. It sends out instructions to your body based upon the code it has been given. This code is the result of your experiences, beliefs and habits that you have developed and they are hard coded into your sub-conscious. While many of us will go through life without changing or upgrading that code, implementing the exercises this book will enable you to make changes to that code. In short you can upgrade your thoughts and actions to meet your needs and desires in your life now.

In order to effectively reprogram your mind, I have developed the MindOS Upgrade System (MUST). This system for upgrading your thinking consists of the following 4 components

1. Purpose
2. Pictures
3. Prose
4. Programme

 **Purpose**

What is your purpose? Easy question but not always a simple answer. Many of us have spent our lives chasing things that we felt were important to us. Maybe you sacrificed everything for your career. Perhaps you were driven by money. Maybe you were driven to have material possessions. These were the things that you thought you wanted. However, when you got all these things you realised that they didn't really make you happy. Does that sound familiar?

This is something I hear so often with my clients. That the things they strived for haven't made them happy. They thought that they would and made many sacrifices to realise these goals. This realisation can lead to deep issues for many people. Often this comes in their mid 40's or early 50's and results in loss of motivation and often anxiety and depression. So, what went wrong?

Well, the reality is that people were chasing substitutes for what they really wanted.

Where do you really want to go?

An example that sticks in my mind of someone in this position is Louise (not her real name). Louise grew up in a deprived part of East London. There was limited expectation in her family, and no one had ever been to University. She heard phrases such as "that's not for people like us" and "don't get ideas above your station." She was however very intelligent and passed the entrance exam to go to her local grammar school. She progressed through life being apparently very successful. She did well at University. She had very responsible jobs in the tech industry. She even got onto the board of a major public company.

I had known Louise for many years. She was one of the hardest working people I knew. She put in very long hours and could always be relied upon. She made huge sacrifices in her personal life for her work. However, she never seemed happy. In fact, she was quite a hard person to be around. She didn't seem to enjoy her job at all but put everything into her work. She seemed to go from one job that she didn't enjoy to another. Even though she was good at her work her unhappiness in her work always hindered her relationships at work.

I could see that Louise had ended up doing something because it had seemed like the right thing to do. Given her background she was desperate to prove to herself that she was worthy enough. She never really believed that she was good enough and just kept trying harder. As was common from people with her background she also had a subconscious belief that what she really wanted to do in life was not available to her. She suffered from Imposter Syndrome. Although she was the most experienced and capable member of the Board in Board meetings, she would rarely say a word. She felt no one would listen to her. She felt like she did not really deserve to be in that position.

Now in her 50's she was being made redundant. This turned her life upside down. She knew that she didn't want to go back into a situation that made her unhappy, but she could not conceive that she could do something else.

She needed to take the time without the pressure (that she put on herself) of work. She needed to take time out to work out what she wanted to do with the rest of her life. She was in a place where she had financial security and she had a supportive partner. Her kids were grown up. She had choices and opportunities. Her constraints were all in her mind

There are many good books on this subject such as Simon Sinek's 'Finding Your Why'. However, without needing to read another book in its entirety, here are the key things that you need to do and that I would advise Louise to do.

1. **Think about and then write down the things that make you happy.** What are the things that really give you pleasure and satisfaction? These may be tasks or characteristics of a task that you do. These can be things in your personal life or things in your work. Think of situations at work that you really enjoyed. What was it about the situation that you really liked?

   Even if you are in a job that you really hate, think about aspects of the job that you really do enjoy. If you have a management job that involves lots of things that you dread think about the parts that you do enjoy? Maybe you hate upward management, but you love developing and coaching people. Maybe you hate internal meetings, but you love meeting customers. Write it down!

2. **What do people say you are great at?** We all have strengths and weaknesses. What are you good at? Even more importantly what do the people who know you well say you are good at. These are your gifts. The things that come easily to you. You may be good at these things because you have had a lot of practice. You may be good at these because it is something that you enjoy. Write these things down.

3. **What things in life do you do for free?** Maybe you teach

kids how to play a sport. Maybe you run a Scout Group. Maybe you volunteer in a charity shop. If you are doing this for free it is certain this is an activity that you love.

It may not be feasible for you to become a professional sports coach or a paid Scout Group Leader. However, you can identify what it is about this voluntary work that gives you satisfaction. Is it the teaching? Is it the organisation? Is it the working with children? Write these things down

Now you know what you enjoy, what you are good at and what you would do for free you can really begin to think about what your future options that might make you happy really are. If you can combine tasks you enjoy, with things you are good at and things that you would do for free you have a good basis for thinking about your future direction.

By combining your skills and your passions you can find something that you will enjoy and be good at.

I am sure that many of you who have been working a long time found yourselves in jobs or careers for one or more of the following reasons

1. It just happened. It was not planned. You fell into doing something.
2. It seemed like a sensible thing to do. Your parents, teachers or you felt that this was a sensible and safe career path to take
3. It was all that was available to you. Everyone in my

town or my school went to work in this factory/ office etc.

Do those scenarios sound familiar? Most people ended up doing what they do for at least one of these reasons. You maybe grew up in an age where you had less options than exist today. Your parents or teachers probably saw job security or a 'safe' career as the most important guidance that they could do for you. They grew up in an age of scarcity, so this was very logical thinking, and it was good advice at the time.

However, we now live in a different time. We have a much more diverse economy. We have careers in fields that never existed before. We can work remotely. In fact, now the problem is almost exactly the opposite of what we had before. There is so much choice it is bewildering. It's a bit like when you turn on the TV there are about 300 channels, but there doesn't seem like anything is worth watching. When you were a child you probably always found something to watch when you just had 3 or 4 Channels.

Exercise 4. Build Yourself a Job or a Role Description

You have all seen those job descriptions that are asking for the impossible? A long list of qualifications that is more like a wish list. Now it is time for you to turn the tables. Write down your own wish list. What is it that you need in a job? What sort of company do you want to work for?

Alternatively, if career is not a priority for you write down your ideal Life Description instead of a job description.

Several years ago, I applied for an internal promotion in the company I was working for. It was a big promotion that would have put me on the board of a major company. I convinced myself that I really wanted the job. I did not get the job. I was devastated at the time. However, looking back now I can see that it was not the right job for me. I liked the idea of the promotion and everything that went with that. The reality was however that this job would have taken me away from doing the things I loved doing and the things I was good at. It would have involved spending a lot more time doing things that I hated.

I loved being with customers. I loved working with my team in the field. I enjoyed mentoring my team. I liked variety. This job was very internal. It would have involved constant upward reporting, lots of internal meetings and global conference calls. It would have involved lots of internal politics with people I found difficult. I would have hated it and been very unhappy doing it.

My manager was great. She could see I was upset. She really valued me however and recognised what I was good at her. She said to me "Jonathan, why don't you write your own job description" Tell us what you want to do. I thought at the time that this was just some sort of 'fob off' to placate me. Now I can see that this was wonderful management and was an open door for me to get what would have been much a much more fulfilling and sustainable role.

Sadly, I was in a place, maybe from conditioning, to believe that success looked like getting that promotion, climbing the corporate ladder until you get to the top rung. The reality is that the top rungs of that ladder are precarious places, what's more there are people all around trying to knock you off that ladder. The guy who got the job could not deal with the pressure and lasted less than a year.

So, whatever your situation right now, write down your ideal Job Description. If you are in a role you have become bored with maybe you can define a role that will keep you in the organisation (or even making the same job more rewarding). If you are at the beginning of your career write down your skills, your passions and what people say you are good at. Make that the basis for deciding what career or job you will be happy and successful in.

If you are looking for a career change do the same thing but add in the experiences that you have gained so far. This will help give you a clear view of not just what you want to do but also how you can utilise your previous experience to give you a head start in your new career.

For example, if you are currently a middle manager in a large company but you decide that you want to retrain to be a therapist, why not specialise in helping people in middle management who have lost their mojo? It will make you relevant and give you a clear niche to focus upon.

Too many people who want to make changes in their life focus only on what they are escaping. They hate the job so much they just want to get away. However, in order to avoid just repeating the same mistake with your next job you really need to ensure you understand what it is you want. When you combine what you enjoy, what you are good at and what you have experience of your future direction becomes much more obvious. Most importantly it becomes achievable.

 **Pictures. Creating an Image of Your Future**

Remember in Section 2.4.1 where we talked about how your mind is a computer? Instead of having a keyboard however your mind has its own 'input' devices. The input 'commands' that your mind responds to are the pictures that you give it the words that you use and the repetition that creates habits. In this section we will focus on how you can develop these powerful enabling images.

Pictures really do speak louder than words for most people. Have you ever watched a movie of a favourite book and been disappointed by the film? This is very common. When we read a book that we like we create our own images. We have a vision in our mind of how the characters look and how the places look. We also do our own 'reading between the lines' in how we interpret the things that are not written down. When we see a movie, we are watching the Directors Interpretation of how they see the characters and the unspoken elements.

No matter how good the Director or the actors are if the movie differs from how we imagined the scene it will be a disappointment to us.

Since the dawn of time humans have realised the power of images to influence how we think. Long before we had words or languages people in caves used pictures to educate. Stories were told through pictures to inform, warn and inspire.

Top sports people used the power of visualisation extensively. Top golfers are constantly visualising every aspect of their game.

Footballers visualise themselves timing their runs to perfection. Boxers see themselves moving freely around the ring. I worked with a football manager who wanted his team to develop visual muscle memory of moving together in unison to maintain their shape during the game. Constantly giving our mind visual instructions will lead our mind to develop the habits that will get us towards our goals. Our minds have muscle memory.

When Roger Bannister broke the seemingly impossible 4 - minute mile barrier in 1954 he relied heavily on visualisation. He saw himself going over the finishing line in less than 4 minutes, seeing and hearing the crowd roaring him on. He even carried a piece of paper in his running shoe with 3.58 written on it. Every other runner had a psychological barrier about breaking this record. He convinced his mind that for him it was possible and saw himself doing it. Once that barrier was broken many more people smashed through it. People could literally now see that it was possible

Now you may not want to break a world record, but you will undoubtedly have your own goals that you want to attain. Seeing yourself attaining these goals will help your subconscious mind to believe this is possible. When your subconscious really believes this it will become easier to take the actions that are necessary to get to that point.

There is significant research that shows visualisation is often more effective than actual practice in making improvements in performance. According to research from Vanderbilt University in 2015.

"Mental imagery can have powerful training effects on behaviour, but how this occurs is not well understood. Here we show that even a single instance of mental imagery can improve attentional selection of a target more effectively than actually practicing visual search. By recording subjects' brain activity, we found that these imagery-induced training effects were due to perceptual attention being more effectively focused on targets following imagined training."

In exercise 6 I cover visualising yourself in your future state. This process of seeing yourself in the place is very powerful. Even more powerful is seeing what you need to do as a process. Whether that is in sporting performance or making a presentation, the more you visualise the process the more that you commit the process to your muscle memory.

Let's now look at the second element of what makes up beliefs, thoughts and actions that guide our subconscious response.

 **Prose. The Words You Use**

Remember how I talked about "sticks and stones" in Chapter 2? "Sticks and Stones may break my bones but calling names won't hurt me." As we know, others consistently calling you names will certainly hurt you.

You as an individual have the same choices. You can choose to use the power of words for good or for bad in your own life and of those around you. You can inspire or depress yourself. You can inspire or inhibit those around you. The words you use are commands to your mind. They are like keyboard stokes that you input into the software of your computer. Your mind doesn't judge whether the command is right. It simply follows your command without question.

The right words can make you improve, can get others to follow you. The wrong words can demotivate you and the others around you. I have a video on my You Tube Channel that shows the incredible power of the right words. You might want to check it out on my YouTube Chanel at youtube.com/myfitmind

For those of you not online let me explain the scenario. It is one of my live events and I ask for a volunteer to come up on stage. I get a few hands and I choose the strongest looking man in the room. I ask him to stand in front of me and I explain what I am going to do. I ask him to put his arm straight out in front of him and then close his eyes. I tell him that I am going to ask him to close his eyes and repeat a phrase 3 times. I then tell him that as he says those words I am going to try and push his arm down and that he should resist me pushing.

He raised his arm and I tell him to repeat the words "I feel very weak" 3 times out loud and to say it like he means it. He says these words and I push down on his arm. His arm goes right down with minimal resistance.

I then tell him that I am going to repeat the exercise with different words. He puts his arm out straight and I ask him to say "I feel incredibly strong" 3 times. I go to push his arm down but this time the resistance is very strong. I push his arm, in the same place with all my might but it keeps bouncing back up again.

Just by using different words so much changed. His ability to resist me was multiplied many times. What was also noticeable was the change in his demeanour. When he kept repeating how weak he was, his shoulders slumped, his breathing was shallower, and his voice sounded less confident. When he was telling himself, he was stronger his shoulders rolled back, and his chest pumped out. His voice was much stronger, and he was breathing more deeply.

Everyone in the room is always amazed when I do this. People are trying to work out 'what the trick is'. There is no trick and I encourage people to do this at home. Kids especially love this. It is a great way of encouraging children to think about the words that they use. If saying these words can have such a significant effect on your strength in that moment, just imagine for a second the relative impact of continually using negative words versus continually using positive words.

Clarity is Key

It is vital to give clear commands to your mind. Just like a programmer writing computer code the quality of the command is vital to the quality of the outcome. Poorly written computer code confuses the computer, taking longer to process and resulting in the system hanging or crashing. Have you ever had that spinning circle of death on your computer? When you give confusing or poor instructions to your brain you get the same effect.

You must give your mind clear and consistent commands. Any ambiguity or lack of consistency will get your mind in a spin and lead to freezing, avoidance or confusion. As Marisa Peer teaches, we must give our minds military style direction so that it is in no doubt what you want from it. She uses this to great effect in her RTT Therapy approach discussed here.

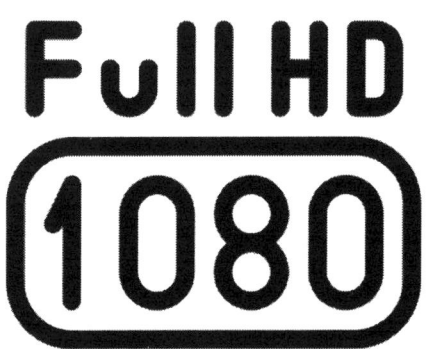

Your mind thrives on clear instructions

What sort of confusing words are you giving your mind? Let me give you some classic examples.

"I want to lose weight, but I love chocolate too much"

"I want to give up drinking, but drinking helps me escape from my pain"

"I am going to try and see if I can do that"

"I might be there"

When you use these phrases, here is what your mind really hears

What you say	What your mind hears
"I'd like to lose weight but I love chocolate too much"	"You love chocolate. You are not serious about losing weight"
"I want to give up drinking but drinking helps me escape from my pain"	"Drinking makes your life tolerable. Keep doing it"
"I am going to try and see if I can do that"	"No you are not. Don't bother"
"I might be there"	"You have no intention of going. You can make an excuse at the last minute for your no show"

Do you ever find yourself saying these things?

"I mustn't forget to take that with me"

"Don't forget your keys"

"Don't lose it"

Expressions like this are too confusing for your mind. It doesn't understand double negatives. It just hears negative. Don't is negative, forget is negative, lose is negative. It hears you shouting all these negatives at it. So, these phrases become

What you say	What your mind hears
"I mustn't forget to take that with me"	"Forget it"
"Don't forget your keys"	"Forget them"
"Don't lose it"	"Lose it"

So, what should you say? You need to give clear, unambiguous commands. Replace double negatives with a positive. Also make words action orientated. So, taking the phrases above here are the correct commands to give your mind (if you really want to do these things

What you say	What you need to say
"I'd like to lose weight, but I love chocolate too much"	"I am going to reduce my weight"
"I want to give up drinking but drinking helps me escape from my pain"	"I am teetotal"
"I am going to try and see if I can do that"	"I will do this" and ideally say when you will do it.
"I might be there"	"I will be there" or "I will see you there. I look forward to it"

Did you notice a few things happening there? We lost the

negative words. We lost the double negatives. We also lost the word lose. Lose is a negative word it rarely has any positive associations. So, when I work with people who come to me for help with losing weight, we find alternatives to the word loss.

Let's see how this works with the next set of phrases now

What you say	What you need to say
"I mustn't forget to take that with me"	"I will remember to take that"
"Don't forget your keys"	"I will remember my keys"
"Don't lose it"	"Put that somewhere safe" or "Keep that safe"

The Words of Others

Our minds respond to the words that we hear. The words that you give it and the words that you hear from others. You have now learnt about the importance of your own words and how you can ensure that you give yourself the right commands. We also however are influenced by the words of others. As discussed earlier the things that others say to us or about us when we are children can have a significant impact on how we think, feel and act later in life.

I see hundreds of clients every year suffering with anxiety or lack of confidence that all began with how they were made to feel about themselves as children. People often carry these beliefs about themselves throughout their life.

Most people carry these feelings through their life. As a result, they may suffer with anxiety, depression and low self-esteem. They find themselves self-sabotaging, procrastinating and avoiding. They may well suffer physical illnesses such as breathing issues, skin problems or autoimmune diseases. It doesn't however have to be that way.

 **Programme**

Your mind is a computer. It comes with an operating system that tells it what to do in each situation. This operating system is partly what you were born with but is then optimised (or limited) by your childhood experiences and environment. Unlike off the shelf operating systems like IOS or Windows however your mind is highly customisable.

For many that customisation begins early in your childhood. You take on board your environment, your company and your experiences to set beliefs, expectations and set your limitations. In the first eight years of your life your mind is extremely receptive and will take on board all these environmental and experiential factors to turn that evolving software code into a hard code operating system. This operating system then guides your thoughts, actions and outcomes as your deep-seated sub-conscious beliefs.

As you know however from earlier in this book, when you understand how, it is possible to change this Program. You can change this Program to reflect what you need it do in your life now and how you want it to function in the future.

Change Your Program
Exercise 5 - Write Down What You Want to Change

Write down the three most important things that you want to change in your life right now. These need to be emotions, behaviours or thoughts that you really want to change. These are your objectives.

Then write down – next to each of these three things, how you would like to feel, think or act differently. These are your 'as is' or how you are now states and your 'to be' or how you want to be states.

To help create that 'to be' image, picture yourself in the future, thinking, feeling and acting how you would like to be. Just picture yourself being there. Close your eyes. See yourself there. How do you feel? What is different. Experience the feeling of how you would like your life to be.

Remember what we learned earlier in this Chapter about the importance of giving yourself clear commands? To create this future, you need to give yourself clear and unambiguous commands. These commands need to be simple and they need to be positive. If you are anxious and you want to be less anxious you need to use a command such as "I am relaxed" or "I am calm".

Here is an example of the 'as is and to be' scenarios. On the left is what you are feeling now and on the right is how you would like to think, feel or act differently in the future

As Is (where you are now)	To Be (where you want to be)
I am anxious about meeting new people	I enjoy meeting new people
I don't feel I can express my opinion	I freely express my opinions
I sabotage myself	I seize my opportunities

Exercise 6. See yourself in this better future

It is powerful to write down these thoughts about what you want to achieve. It gives your mind an aiming point. It helps your mind to begin the process of understanding what you really want.

When you have written these goals down find a quiet place to sit. Now just close your eyes, pay attention to your breathing and be aware of the weight of your body on the chair or furniture. Take 30 -60 seconds to do this and feel yourself relaxing.

Then, in your mind, picture yourself in the future, feeling the way you want to feel. Depending upon your specific objectives you may find it easier to focus on just 1 or 2 of your 'to be' goals.

Focus on picturing yourself in that 'to be' situation. If you are currently anxious about meeting others as in the example above, then picture yourself meeting strangers in the future. See yourself being relaxed, being happy, being excited to meet new people. See yourself smiling, looking and feeling very relaxed. Now 'feel' how it feels to be in that situation. Notice the feelings in your body. How does it feel? How does it feel different or better to how it has felt in the past? Take as much time as you need to 'feel' yourself in this place. What are you seeing? Most importantly focus on the physical sensations that you are experiencing.

Perhaps you will notice that your demeanour is better. Maybe you stand taller. Maybe your shoulders are more relaxed. Perhaps your voice seems stronger and clearer. You probably feel much less tense. Maybe your muscles are so much looser. Possibly your breathing is slower and deeper.

Whatever is your 'to be' just observe how much better it feels compared to how it feels in your 'as is' state. Notice the feelings in your body. See what you see, hear what you hear and most importantly, feel what you are feeling in the 'to be' future state.

Did you notice that change? So did your mind. You are beginning to give it a message about your future direction. Your mind wants you to be happy. It wants to give you what you want.

Exercise 7. Write Down Your Script

Now that you have identified how you want to feel and 'felt' that feeling you need to write the software code that will enable your mind to change the commands that you are giving yourself.

Don't worry. You do not need to have any software coding skills. With some guidance from me you need to develop a script that will give you the new coding. This is a bit like being a Hollywood Actor where you need to have your lines in order to truly get into your new character. However, you get to write your own lines. How cool is that? Even Hollywood A lister's don't get to write their own scripts.

Don't worry if that sounds daunting. I am going to help you. I have provided a script template for you at Appendix A. All you must do is fill in the gaps to make this script very personal for you. You just need to do some personalisation for you. This is very important and very powerful. Let me explain why.

Many people who come to me say they have listened to hypnosis recordings before. These are typically recordings for anxiety, weight loss or maybe smoking. Most people say that they find them helpful, but they don't really give them the shift that they were looking for. This is because these recordings are generic. A one size fits all. When I do a one-to-one session with a client, I make them a totally personalised recording to listen to. I tailor the recording to focus on exactly what they want to hear. Equally importantly, I also make sure that I use words that are meaningful and personal to that client.

These personalised recordings are hugely effective in programming your mind because your mind feels that you are talking to it directly. You are saying things that really resonate and are using words that that are very personal. This makes your mind buy into what it is hearing and take away resistance. It is trusting in what its hearing.

Of course, I can't give you a totally personalised recording within a book but what I can do is give you a proven structure in Appendix A that works, as with these generic recordings but with your own personalisation.

To develop your own personalised script, you need to take your objectives that you developed in Exercise 5 above and use these to fill in the gaps. In the script. You then have your own, personalised hypnotherapy script.

I recommend that you print off this script and write down those outcomes in the gaps. Read through the script to make sure that it flows and make sense for you.

Remember to make sure that your objectives are positive and affirmative. Do not use any negatives or double negatives.

When you are comfortable with your script read it out loud and record it. Speak slowly and clearly in a steady 'hypnotic voice'. A hypnotic voice is a slow, steady voice, with little change in tone of voice. You don't need any fancy equipment. Any smartphone will have a voice recorder where you can easily record as an MP3 file

Like anything new this may take a bit of practice. That is a good thing. The act of writing down what you want, reading it and listening back to it is very powerful. You are beginning the process of telling your mind what it needs to hear in order to move forward.

Your final recording should be around 10 minutes long. In the next Chapter I am explain the process you need to follow to listen to this recording, in order to get maximum results.

You will need to listen to this recording every day for 21 days. In 21 days, you will have developed new habits of thought. The things that you want to believe (those goals that I asked you to write down) will overwrite the thoughts that were holding you back.

Need help?

Some people say to me that they don't like to hear their own voice or that they are finding it to time consuming to make their own recording. I do offer a service to provide this recording for you. Simply email me at jonathan.butler@myfitmind.co.uk I will provide you with details of how to receive your own personalised and powerful hypnosis recording.

Chapter 5

Step 4
Re-enforce Your New Habits and Beliefs

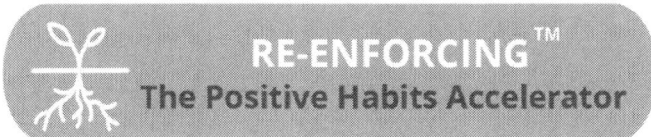

In Step 3 you learned the principles of how to reprogram you mind. I taught you about how we use words and pictures to change the way we think. I showed you how to develop a script for your own personalised hypnosis recording.

As you know by now your mind is like a computer. As well as giving ourselves words and pictures to reprogram ourselves we also learn to change behaviours through the creation of new habits. We also need to enable our new, helpful habits to take deep roots and flourish.

There are 4 elements to this re-enforcement process that will allow you to embed the new beliefs and behaviours. Addressing each of these elements is key to making the change stick.

Based upon my experience of delivering lasting change I have developed *the Positive Habits Accelerator*. This tool allows you to ensure that you are giving yourself the environment and the opportunity to make your change deep and lasting. The Positive Habits Accelerator has 4 Components. These are

1. **R**outine
2. **R**elationships
3. **R**epelling
4. **R**ewards

 **Routine and The Power of Habits**

You may have heard people use phrases such as artificial intelligence or machine learning. These are phrases that are used to describe how computers are learning to be 'intelligent' in order to predict what we want. If you are not aware of these phrases or are aware but are not sure what they mean you are almost certainly experiencing them. If you shop on Amazon for example have you noticed how it brings up recommendations for you? The Amazon software is looking into its memory to judge what it thinks you like. Maybe if you bought something consumable like printer ink, it may well suggest, after a period of time that you buy a replacement.

Or perhaps you have a smart phone. When you write texts or emails it suggests words or even phrases for you. You may have noticed how much more sophisticated and personalised this has become. This is because the software learns that you use certain words or phrases and begins to second-guess you.

Your brain works the same way. If we consistently do or say

certain things these become habits. Maybe you always need a cup of coffee at a certain time or maybe you always take the same route to work. Maybe you like to sleep on one side of a bed. These are all habits.

Repetition creates powerful habits

A habit is when our subconscious mind makes us do something without any conscious thought. Habits can be very powerful. There have been some great books written about this such Steven Covey's '7 Habits of Highly Effective People

I was on a Zoom call just the other day with Daniel Priestley, Best Selling Author of Key Person of Influence. Daniel was talking also about the importance of habit for being successful in our lives and careers. He coined a phrase that I loved. He said that 'consistency always beats intensity.' I can tell you as someone who writes books and develops online courses that this consistency is critical for anyone who wants to make any kind of shift in their life.

They say that everybody has a book inside them but seeing a book through to completion is a major undertaking. It takes a long time, it requires dealing with boredom, loss of inspiration, the distractions of daily life and self-doubt.

While everybody may have a great idea or expertise to share not everyone is going to (or want to write a book). Should you wish to write and complete book the key thing you need to do is to establish and make a habit the Routine of writing. Established writers will have a routine for writing. They will set aside blocks of time for writing. They will probably have a particular place, they may turn their phones off and tell their family not to disturb them during these times.

With any big objective or project, we must 'slice the elephant' or the task just seems too big. Once we create that routine however, we start to see progress and that motivates us to continue. We are going to slice the elephant of reprogramming your mind by committing 20 minutes a day for 21 days to taking on board your new habits of belief

Creating Your Habit of Belief

To form a new habit or routine takes just 21 days. That applies equally to creating your new habits of belief. What do I mean by that? I mean embedding the new commands (the words and pictures from your recording) into your subconscious mind

To create your new habits of belief you now need to listen to your recording for 21 days. Hearing the words that you want to hear about yourself, consistently, is critical to enabling you to embed those new beliefs of thought, habit and action that you want to have.

Your recording should be approximately 15 minutes long and you need to create a routine of listening to this recording. Here are

3 things you need to do to create the perfect environment to listen to you recording

1. **Set a time every day that you will listen,** without fail, to the recording. Ideally this should be last thing at night. This is the perfect time as your brain is very receptive in this moment and because it is very powerful to wake up with the last words and pictures in your head being empowering and uplifting thoughts.

2. **Make sure you are relaxed and unlikely to be disturbed.** Last thing at night in bed also makes this a great time. Kids should be asleep; you are unlikely to be disturbed by phone calls and the messages of modern life. Bed is a great place because you should be relaxed and because you can fall asleep while you are listening to the recording. It is perfectly okay to fall asleep.

   You should discuss with your partner and get their support to do this. You also need to find a time and space that works for you. You don't want to worry about being disturbed by a partner's snoring as you listen to the recording. Also, I do not want to disrupt anyone's sex life! That is a very important part of a relationship so just find a time and place to listen that works for you and your relationships

3. **Learn the Spiegel Eye Roll**[7] **for entering deep**

---

[7] The Spiegel Eye Roll is named after Dr Herbert Spiegel, the American Psychiatrist who famously helped combat troops to reduce the pain of injuries on the battlefield using hypnosis. He developed this technique to enter hypnosis quickly and in any situation.

hypnosis. You can simply listen to the recording and be hypnotised by your voice. I would suggest that you lie down or sit comfortably in a chair and follow these steps

1. Start playing the recording from the beginning
2. Be aware of the weight of your body and he contact with the furniture
3. Close your eyes
4. Focus on your breathing. Take steady breaths, through your nose. Just feel the sensation of breathing and focus on your breath. With every in breath be aware of the air entering your lungs. With every out breath just feel yourself letting go.

Here is a technique called the Spiegel eye roll that you can use to make yourself go even deeper into hypnosis and get there very quickly. I have a video of this on my YouTube channel at youtube.com/myfitmind available to my subscribers. So please subscribe and you can see this video. The steps are very simple.

1. At step 3 above, instead of closing your eyes, keep your eyes open
2. Now looking straight ahead, roll up your eyes so you are trying to look into the roof of your eyes. To anyone watching you will look a bit like a zombie as they will pretty much just see the whites of your eyes only. This will feel a bit strange and may be a tiny bit uncomfortable
3. Keep those eyes looking up as you take 3 steady

breaths, through your nose. Just focus on being aware of your breathing

4. After 3 breaths you can close your eyes and let your eyes just come back to a normal position and continue to step 4 above as you listen to the recording.

When you were rolling your eyes up you will probably have felt the need to blink and felt your eyelashes fluttering. This is a good sign. It means you are very easily entering a brain state where you are naturally able to take on board new thoughts and beliefs about yourself. In short, you are highly receptive.

If you fall asleep listening to the recording that is perfectly okay. You will still be absorbing everything that you hear.

 Relationships

We are the average of the 5 people we hang out with, according to motivational speaker Jim Rohn. You can argue about the specifics of averages and 5 people, however the fact is that the people who you spend most time with will have a major impact upon how you think, feel and act.

If you hang out with 'merchants of doom' it is hard to maintain a balanced, positive outlook on life. Similarly, if you hang out with positive, motivated people it is likely to have a positive impact upon you. Environment is so important. As I discussed earlier in the book there is plenty of debate about the relative importance of nature versus nurture in how our life prospects are determined. However, making sure that you spend time with the right people is the one of the most critical things that you can do. It is something that you have significant control over and can make a huge change to how you feel and what you can achieve.

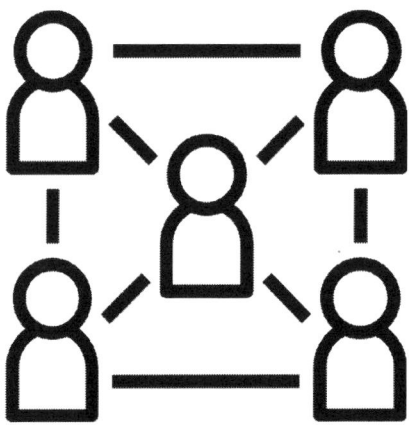

Since the dawn of time likeminded people have gathered. I grew up near the city of Coventry in England. In the early and mid-20th Century Coventry was a world leader in engineering and specifically automotive engineering. At one point there were over 100 car and motorcycle manufacturers in this relatively small city. During WW2 the Nazi's saw that Coventry's industrial output was so critical to the British war effort that Luftwaffe repeatedly bombed the repurposed car factories.

In the boom times manufacturers clamoured to move there. The supply chains moved there. Anybody who was anybody in the British Motor Industry knew they needed to be there, in the company of the brightest and most motivated engineers of the time. It was not just people from the UK either. The founders of Triumph were German engineers who saw the need to be around this energy and sense of momentum. Even Gottlieb Daimler of

Mercedes Benz fame licenced the use of his name and engines to the Coventry based Daimler Company.

Companies we are familiar with today such as Land Rover, Jaguar, Triumph and the London Electric Vehicle Company (makers of the famous London Black Cab) are the result of that meeting of like-minded people and their ideas in one small City in the English Midlands

Similar phenomena happened with the movie industry in California. Today we have Silicon Valley in California with the likes of Apple, Google, Uber, and Zoom etc. In China we have Shenzhen as the hub for inward investment and the Chinese tech industry.

The point is that ambitious and driven people want to be around like-minded people. They can learn, collaborate and seek out opportunity. They raise their game and inspire those who follow them to do the same.

Have you noticed how many top businesspeople or entrepreneurs have been to the worlds leading Universities? So many of these people have been to the likes of Harvard, Yale, Oxford, MIT or Cambridge Universities. Now is it because of what they teach them that they are so successful? Well of course the teaching is good in these places, but did you know the students get a lot less lectures than in most Universities? You know what is the greatest thing student's gain there? It is the connections with the likeminded people. They are mixing with intelligent, motivated people with great expectations. They are in an environment that inspires and provides a platform to achieve. Few of us will have the opportunity to attend such an institution but we can consciously decide to hang out with people who will inspire us, push us forward and that we can learn from.

Do you get the point? The people we hang about with make a huge difference to our thoughts, feelings, well-being and results. The right relationships uplift you; the wrong ones hold you back or drag you down.

Exercise 7. Audit Your Relationships

Are your relationships holding you back or moving you forward? You may not want to be the next Bill Gates or Mark Zuckerberg. You want to be your best, authentic self, however. You want to thrive and be happy in your own field and in your life. So whatever success looks like for you, are you around the right people to help get you and keep you there.

Take a piece of paper or write on your computer a table with 4 Columns. In the first column write down the names of the 5 people that you spend the most time with (excluding your children). In the second column write down on a scale of 1-10 the contribution these people make to helping you be the person you want to be.

If the score is less than 5 these people are a negative influence upon you. If they are more than 5 they are a positive impact upon you.

In the third column write down next to anyone who is a 5 or less whether you have the possibility of replacing or reducing the role of this person in your life

In the fourth column. Write down what action you need to take. If the person is less than 5 and you can cut that person out of your life – write down what you're going to do? If you rated the relationship 5 or less but you cannot realistically change it write down what you can do to reduce the impact of this person or to limit the contact with them.

Person/ Relationship	Contribution to my wellbeing (1-10)	Can I remove easily or change	Action Plan
Fred / Boss	4	No	Understand his style and respond in this way. Not take it personally and accept this is just 'his way'.
Sue/ friend	3	Yes	Make myself unavailable.
Lucy/ friend	8	NA	Spend time I would have spent with Sue
Jason/ colleague	8	NA	Go to lunch together. Ask him for more help
Tracey/ Colleague	2	Yes	Take lunch at different time. Just be polite but don't listen to her or let in her negativity. Feel sorry for her rather than be angry.

If you are serious about making and maintain change you have to either replace the toxic people or find a strategy to deal with them. I work with my private clients to help them deal better with difficult people. I usually find there are 2 kinds of 'difficult people'. Firstly, there are the people with different styles. Secondly there are what I would broadly deem to be those with sociopathic or narcissistic tendencies.

With the first category it is helpful to recognise that sometimes people just have different styles, and it is 'their way'. If you are a talkative person or a detail-oriented person you may well find it hard to relate to people who are very direct or very brief in their communications. That style can be very grating to you.

When you understand that this is just their style and it is not personal it can help you greatly to deal with their approach. If you feel yourself getting annoyed with their approach just keep telling yourself phrases like "it's just their way". Even better is to do what is called a 'pattern interrupt'. When you feel you are going to get annoyed when someone communicates with you in a certain way think of the most ridiculous thing that you can think of. Maybe think of an elephant dancing in a tutu or the person who is annoying you walking around with their pants on their head. The more ridiculous the image you create the more effective this will be. It interrupts the pattern or the cycle and allows you to take back control. If you feel yourself smiling, you know you are doing this right.

Exercise 8. Understand Others Communication Styles

Think of those who you find difficult to deal with. What is it you find difficult about them? Is their style of communicating very different to you? If they are the kind of people who write one-line emails or send texts with a few words, then they are just economical with words. They are typically action oriented, impatient and fast paced people. They will likely struggle with people who talk a lot or write long complicated emails. So, if you have a boss or a customer who has this style learn to adapt to their style. If they are your boss, the reality is that you have you make an accommodation. If they send you a one liner just learn to communicate with them in a similar style and see how the relationship changes. You both get less frustrated with each other and can build a far greater understanding.

Adapt style to overcome conflict

There are some great books on this subject and there is a whole method and training programme called 'Insights' that was developed by Scotsman Andi Lothian that helps people in teams to work better by understanding each other's styles. I thoroughly recommend looking into this if you are dealing with workplace conflict.

Breathing and Anxiety

When we talk negative, we talk ourselves into a bad place. I specialise in helping people to overcome physical symptoms associated with anxiety. I get many people presenting with respiratory problems. People tell me they have Asthma, panic attacks where they struggle to breathe, even Sleep Apnoea. Most anxious people have very shallow breathing. Habitual shallow breathing is almost always present in anxious people.

Now think about this. What happens when you are anxious? You feel tense, your neck and shoulder muscles tighten, your heart rate increases, and your breathing becomes shallow. You are in 'fight, flight or freeze' mode. Being in this survival mode means that your body is just focused on protecting you. It is focusing energy on what you need to do to keep yourself safe in that moment. That is great when you are in an occasional situation where you need to avoid real danger. However, when you are constantly in this condition (a chronic state of anxiety) it means that the rest of your body is being starved of what it needs. You have probably heard about explorers in the Arctic who lose toes or tips of fingers. This is because the body is sensing danger from the extreme cold conditions and is solely focused on maintaining your vital organs. It is the same principle with chronic anxiety.

So, people suffering with breathing problems or skin conditions will typically go to the doctors. The doctor, in the 10 minutes they have will probably prescribe medication to treat the presenting issue. Often, they will prescribe inhalers or nebulizers. These prescriptions may help but they are only dealing with the symptoms. What really needs to be done, is to deal with the anxiety that is underpinning the issue. This is addressing the root cause.

I strongly advise everybody to give more focus to their breathing. It is so important and breathing better will really help so many aspects of your wellbeing. Really be conscious of your breathing. When you feel under pressure notice how your breathing gets shallower. Just catch this. Regulate your breathing, breathe more deeply and just focus your attention for 1-2 minutes on nothing but your breathing. Try doing this while having your bare feet flat on the ground. Really notice that sensation of being connected to the floor.

Repel

There will be people in your life that you cannot bear to be around! This is unavoidable. Personally, I cannot stand arrogant, narcissistic people. The type of people who just want to tell you about themselves. If I meet these types of people socially, I will seek a very quick exit. Being British I will try and do this politely, but I will do it swiftly. I do not have the time or energy to give these people space in my life or to give them a platform to stand on. I simply refuse to be around toxic people.

There will of course be situations when you must deal with these people. If you are in sales, you may have customers like this. If they are an important customer, you are going to have to learn to deal with this. In fact, if you can get yourself into the right state you cannot just deal better with these people but also, they can become good customers. These people like to be listened to. They like to have attention and sadly these types of people are often quite successful in corporate careers as most people internally will never challenge them. If you can listen to these people while your competitors run a country mile then you are likely to win that big deal or get a bigger slice of their business. These people just love to have their ego stroked.

In my business career I had to deal with a lot of people like this. My way of coping with it was to recognise that this was just a business transaction and it would pass. They would never be my friend and I could let their words and actions just bounce off me. Every time I had a meeting or a phone call with one of these people I would smile. I would then visualise that I had a shield around me. I would then visualise that their bullshit words and negative energy would just bounce off my shield. This made me smile more

When I went home at night, I would imagine that I was going back into my castle and that I was pulling up my drawbridge and leaving this person well behind. As a result, if this I became incredibly fussy about who I would spend my personal time with. If my wife suggested, we had dinner with people that I did not like I would just refuse to do it. My personal time was too precious to make polite conversation with people I did not like.

So, when you have a choice about the company you keep, be brutal. You are not doing yourself or the other person a favour by spending time with them. If you don't like them there is a pretty good chance that they don't like you either!

When you must be with somebody that you do not like give yourself that armour. Have your protection. Do what you need to do in your dealings with them. Recognise that they are how they are, and they will not change. Feel sorry for them. If they start to annoy you just picture them with that pair of oversize underpants on their head. Of course, you need to control your amusement if they are right in front of you!

Many years ago, I went on an advanced driving course. The instructor talked to us about how to deal with aggressive or inconsiderate drivers. It is of course so easy to get annoyed by the bad behaviour of others and when we are in our cars. Feeling safe in our metal box on wheels, we can turn into our Reptilian Self, lashing out at others who threaten or inconvenience us. The instructor encouraged us to say out loud "fellow traveller" every time that another driver did something that annoyed us. I am not sure that the instructor knew this, but this was a classic 'pattern interrupt' technique to stop the situation escalating. The words 'fellow traveller' also suggest affinity with the person behind. Instead of the expletives or insults that might come into your mind when someone tailgates you saying fellow traveller somehow felt soothing.

Saying these words gave you back control over the situation. He also suggested that when someone is aggressive in the car you ask yourself questions like. "What is going on in his/her life that they are so angry?" Their presence in your life is so fleeting. In a few moments they will be gone out of your life forever. They do not deserve your time or energy.

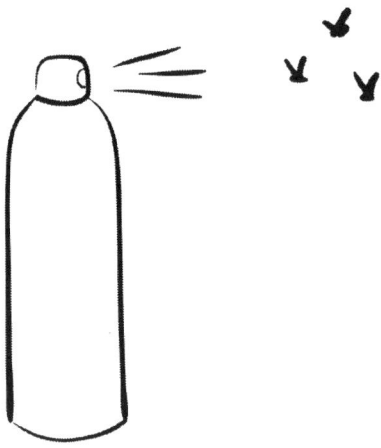

Repel the people who pull you down

As with bullies, aggressive drivers are all about their problems. Their anger, their bad day, their empty lives. If you reframe your reptilian reaction of getting angry into one of pity or even just ambivalence, then see how much better it feels.

Remember that we cannot change everything that happens around us. We can only change how we react to the events that we are faced with. When we recognise this we give ourselves back control. Like everything this requires some practice but as you now understand we can form new habits very quickly. When you find yourself reframing how you see a situation your reactions will change. You will be able to respond and cope in a better, more empowering and less stressful way. Start practicing this and notice how it feels. It feels so good to be able to rise above the situation. It makes you the better person. It gives you control.

In the Vietnam War Admiral Jim Stockdale was the most senior US serviceman to be taken prisoner. He was held in terrible conditions in the prison that became nicknamed 'the Hanoi Hilton'. Stockdale was kept in terrible conditions and tortured regularly by his captors. He recognised that despite his rank there was little he could do to change his situation. So instead, he decided to focus on and judge himself against the things that he could control. The only things he could control were his reactions and he decided that every day he would judge himself by his behaviours in the prison against three criterions. These were what he called his CPD measures. CPD stood for Calm, Personable and Dignified. These were things that he could control and, in every situation, he learned to hold himself accountable for these 3 things.

While others around him died or lost their sanity Stockdale was able to survive and gain immense personal strength in his future life and career from these events. If you are in a situation where you cannot avoid certain toxic people or situations, what are your equivalents of Stockdale's CPD? (Stockdale). Write them down. Keep them in a prominent place and review them everyday.

 **Reward**

Do you ever find that you only look at the negatives? At the end of the day do you beat yourself up about the task that you did not get finished? Do you agonise over mistakes that you made?

This is sadly human nature. If somebody gives us feedback on our work, we don't hear all the good things that they say. We just hear the negative. If there are 5 bits of positive feedback and one piece of negative feedback, we get hung up about the one negative comment.

To some extent this can be helpful because it is true that we do learn far more from mistakes that we do from our successes.

However, if we are so hung up on the mistakes we make or the things that don't work out what do you think happens?

As well as making ourselves feel bad what happens is that in the future we begin to avoid, to procrastinate or to hide. Our mind does not want us to be hurt so we stop taking chances.

The world's most successful people embrace mistakes. Just like young children they learn by trial and error they accept that to make progress we must make mistakes. We learn from mistakes. Every time we make a mistake, we get close to making the breakthrough or progress we want. I strongly recommend that you banish the word failure from your vocabulary and replace it with learning.

Steve Jobs, Marie Curie, James Dyson, Elon Musk, Serena Williams, Christiano Ronaldo got where they did by trying things and learning from their mistakes. They tried and they learned until they succeeded. Just like we do as children. We learn to walk by falling over and getting up again. Children don't think of falling over as failure, it is just part of the learning process. No great achievement is ever accomplished by taking the easy route. In life we learn, and we succeed. The only failure is not to try.

It is so important to reward yourself for your achievements. It drives you on. It makes you feel good. It gives you energy. Rewards do not have to be big. Rewarding yourself can simply be telling yourself 'well done'. Maybe you have had a job to do in the house that you have been putting off for months. When you do this job say, 'well done'.

We know how important it is to reward children rather than punish them. It's the same with animals too. If you want to change behaviour encourage the outcome that you want rather than punishing the outcome that you don't want. It is just the same for us. Make yourself feel good for the things you do. Give them more emphasis than the things we don't do.

Exercise 9. Reflect on Your Day

Here is what I do last thing at night. As I go to bed, I recall the things I have achieved during the day. I only think of the good things. I congratulate myself on what I have done. It doesn't have to be a massive thing. It could just be an action, or it could be how I reacted to a difficult situation.

Congratulate yourself if you have rung a friend or family member that you have not spoken to for ages. Maybe you sorted out some admin. Maybe you helped a stranger in the street. Just be happy for what you have done. Feel how it feels to reflect just on the positive as you go to sleep

Further Help

I hope that you have enjoyed this book. I have sought to provide as much as is possible in a self-help book. I have share teachings that you can implement yourself to make real and lasting changes in your life.

If you enjoyed this book please do leave me a review on Amazon. You can simply leave the review on the order page. Here is the link to follow online

https://www.amazon.co.uk/review/create-review/?channel=glance-detail&asin=B08XJT9TDQ&ie=UTF8&

Should you wish to learn more there are several options

1. Subscribe to my mailing list to get exclusive offers and access to new material. Simply provide your name and email to this link http://eepurl.com/gzWYk5
2. RTT Therapy and Coaching, globally via Zoom and in person. I offer free introductory Discovery Calls. You can book these from my website at www.myfitmind.co.uk
3. You can go to my website, my Facebook page or my YouTube channel to see regular updates and advice.

www.myfitmind.co.uk

www.facebook.com/myfitmind

www.youtube/myfitmind

Acknowledgements

I would like to give my thanks to the following people, without whom this book would never have been possible.

To Marisa Peer for giving me the courage to change my career direction, for teaching me and trusting me to practice her wonderful Rapid Transformational Therapy technique

To my son Louie for being such a great son and inspiration to me

To Tais for introducing me to different ways of thinking about wellbeing.

To Andy Harrington for showing me how to turn my ideas into this book and my courses.

To Ali Campbell for deepening my understanding of hypnosis techniques

To David Bandler for developing NLP and sharing his knowledge with the world

To my sister Andrea for being a great support to me in the last few years as I made this transition

To my brother Steve for helping me catch up with the world of digital marketing

To my Mum and Dad for bringing me into the world

Last but certainly not least to, my clients for putting their trust in me and helping me learn every day about human behaviour.

Worksheets and hand-outs

Appendix A. Increased Confidence Hypnosis Script

Instructions

1. Insert your own words in the 4 places where it says <insert your own words>. These words should follow the style and tone of the other words but reflect what is in important for you. Make these words personal to you and reflect how you want to see yourself thinking, feeling and acting in the future. It may be that you want to describe a very particular situation such as public speaking, an interview or having the confidence to approach the opposite sex
2. If you are focused on a particular issue (such as being confident in an interview) I suggest that you repeat your own sentence in each of the 4 places.
3. Speak calmly and clearly in an assertive voice.
4. Pause for 1-2 seconds between each paragraph but feel free to pause as feels natural to you
5. Sprinkle the use of your name throughout the script. This makes it even more personal to you

The Script

Make yourself comfortable. Place your feet flat on the floor and your hands separated, on your lap. Be aware of the weight of your body and your contact with the furniture.

Now, keep your head level but raise your eyes and look up as high as you possibly can. It is as if you are looking into your eyebrows. And now that you are looking up, fix your gaze at an overhead spot so that your eyes are straining just a little and keep looking at that spot. Breathe in, hold it a while and then breathe out slowly.

Take another inward breath, hold it in and breathe out slowly. Now just take one more breath, holding it in for longer this time, and as you exhale slowly close your eyelids. As your eyelids close, you notice that the muscles and nerves in and around your eyes are becoming heavy, droopy, drowsy, and now just forget all about your eyes. Just allow a drifting, floating feeling to develop in your body, just let that drifting, floating feeling take over.

Now picture that you are standing at the top of a staircase with 10 steps. These are very beautiful and gentle steps that are just so easy to descend. Now picture a place where you love to be. This is a place where you feel happy, safe and carefree. This is a place where anything is possible. Just see yourself in that place. See what you see in that place, hear what you hear and feel what you feel in that wonderful place.

Now lower your chin and look down to this wonderful place. You are getting the sensation you might get as you look over a balcony. You're looking down 10 steps. You have that looking down sensation right now. You're moving on to step 10 as each muscle, every nerve turns loose, lets loose, and you go deeper. You're taking step 9 and you can feel your feet treading each step. You're taking step 8; you can hear your feet contacting every step as you go deeper. You're taking step 7, you can see your feet moving on to every step as you go deeper, into an awareness of yourself. You're taking step 6 now as each muscle, every nerve turns loose, lets loose, and you go deeper. You're taking step 5, you're halfway down, drifting and floating deeper. You're taking step 4, going even deeper. You're taking step 3, as each muscle, every nerve, turns loose, lets loose, and you go deeper. You're taking step 2, as you gently, calmly, easily move into an even deeper sleep of the mind. You're taking the final step, and just let yourself go deeper as you feel a drifting, floating feeling.

Just allow that drifting, floating feeling to continue. You are aware that you are not aware, you are listening but you are not listening as you go deeper, you are concentrating with your subconscious mind while your conscious mind just drifts away. Deeper means being able to have the most wonderful relaxation and insight - so just let you go deeper. Let yourself go deeper, and as you go deeper, as you go deeper with every breath you take, just think about how you want to see yourself. See yourself becoming more confident. And how you will be as you become more confident, what a difference that will make to your life being more confident. See how you walk and how you stand. See how you would enter a room.

You notice that your arms are feeling heavy. So heavy. The harder you try to lift them the heavier they feel.

As you go deeper you are aware already of a change taking place in you. You are realising that you have an ability to release tremendous confidence. As you go deeper just see yourself the way you want to be. Just focus on how you want to be. You are focusing on how you are becoming. Knowing that what you see and focus on, your mind will move towards what you want. Your mind is like a heat seeking missile, programmed to take you towards that which you focus on. You are focusing on being confident. You are directing and commanding your mind. You have the power to choose how you are going to think and act and feel, and you are choosing to move towards greater and greater confidence.

You were born with super high self-esteem, with a great amount of confidence, with a tremendous belief in yourself. You still have that confidence that you were born with. It has been waiting to be re-ignited, restarted re-launched. As you go deeper, you are becoming aware of more and more confidence inside you. You like yourself more. Other people like you. You can make the right decisions for yourself. Every day you are becoming more and more self-assured, more self-trusting and much more secure within yourself. You can trust your own judgments.

As you go deeper, you are aware that you are believing in yourself more and more every day and you can express your thoughts, needs and emotions freely. You are developing more and more confidence in yourself as you go deeper, you are aware that as you are developing more confidence in yourself, other people are developing more confidence in you. As you appreciate yourself it is easier for other people to appreciate you more. You express your emotions with ease and honesty. You are honest with yourself and with others. You are becoming more confident every day.

As you go deeper you are aware that you have a strong desire, a powerful motivation to be your most confident self. You believe in yourself. You love yourself for who you are. You give love to others and you accept it with ease. You easily accept yourself as a lovable and likeable person. People like you and you like them. You're at ease around people, they respond well to your confidence, to your warmth, to your personality. Your body, your mind working together in perfect harmony, motivating you to move, think, act and react with tremendous confidence.

<Insert your own words

....
....
....
....>

As you go deeper you are free to believe in yourself, to be yourself, to like yourself. Every part of you is more confident than ever before. In new situations you find your breathing is deep and steady, your voice is clear, you make eye contact, and you move in an easy way. Your radiate positive energy, your actions are positive, you are confident. You are relaxed, open and at ease. You make people want to be around you

As you go deeper, you're at ease. You recognise that you can't control every event that happens in life, but you trust yourself to react in the right way, to take any event in your stride. You have an innate ability to put those around you at ease.

You can realise your potential. You radiate belief and confidence, which rubs off on others around you. You know you are talented and unique just by being you. You believe in yourself. You are enthusiastic about being you. About living your life. You radiate confidence. You're able now to surpass your own expectations and surpass the expectations from others.

<Insert your own words

....
....
....
....>

As you go deeper you truly do believe in yourself. You have choices and power now and this is reflected in your own strong, confident voice. You accept that the most important words you ever hear are the words you say to yourself. The most important opinion for you is your own opinion. And your opinion of yourself is getting stronger, more positive every day. You are aware that you are instructing your mind clearly and therefore you are directing your life. As a child other people directed you and you were dependent on them for your feelings about yourself. But you are directing yourself and your life now, and you won't allow anyone to lessen or diminish this control and direction you have over your life and your feelings. Confidence is taking root in you now and every day you are becoming more confident, more resilient, more at ease in every situation. You now see problems as opportunities. You feel easily able to deal with whatever life deals you and you easily overcome every challenge with enthusiasm and belief in yourself.

You have an infinite capacity to change, and you're using your imagination to see yourself, to be the way you want to be. You radiate supreme confidence in new situations, around people. You sound confident and you feel confident. You project this confidence, self-trust and self-assuredness. You have absolute confidence; you can handle any and every situation that you meet.

<Insert your own words

....
....
....
....>

You like people and people like you back. Each day you are feeling more and more confident. Your self-esteem and self-image are higher than ever before. You are discovering your talents and abilities. Every day you feel more confident, and you can handle any situation. You think clearly, you act positively. . And as you go deeper now, you can see yourself in your brilliant future. As you speak to others your breathing is deep and steady. Your voice is clear and strong. Your body language is positive. You instinctively know what to do in any situation.

<Insert your own words

....
....
....
....>

Going deeper now you see yourself the way you want to be, the way you are determined to be. You have tremendous faith in your ability to achieve what you want to achieve. You have faith in yourself and in your decisions. You are confident; you move and communicate with confidence. Your increased confidence is enhancing every area of your life- your relationships, your feelings about yourself, your realtionships, your career, and your achievements. You can let go of the past; feel good about the present and to have high expectations for your future.

Your mind easily accepts every word it is hearing. You listen to this recording every day. Each day you are becoming more and more aware of the powerful impact that these w more confident.

Should you listen to this recording last thing at night you will fall asleep and have the most wonderful night's sleep. You will be deeply embedding these beliefs about yourself as you sleep. You will have the most energising and refreshing night's sleep. You will wake up feeling renewed, refreshed and re-invigorated. You will wake up bursting with energy and belief, excited and motivated about whatever the day has in store.

>OR For listening in the daytime replace the last paragraph with the following paragraph to finish<

So just take a few moments in silence and once more focus on how you want to be. Focus on how you are becoming. See yourself confident in any situation. I'm going to bring you back to your full awareness now. On the count of 1, you are returning to full awareness feeling wonderful. On the count of 2 you are feeling calm, relaxed at ease, knowing this feeling will stay with you. On the count of 3 you are feeling perfect in every way, physically, mentally, emotionally perfect, perfectly able to be more confident than ever before. On the count of 4, feeling motivated, feeling refreshed and on the count of 5, wide awake and feeling great.

A

Alcohol, 17
Anxiety, 4, 6, 1, 5, 22, 86
Associations, 6, 16, 17, 18
Audit, 7, 82
Automatic Negative Thought, 20, 39, 41
Automatic Negative Thoughts, 39, 40

B

Brain, 9, 25
Breathing, 86
Bruce Lipton, 4

C

Carol Dweck, 4
CBT, 2
Chimp Paradox, 2
Clarity, 61
Commands, 11, 13
Confidence, 1, 4, 97, 102
Counselling, 2
Coventry, 80, 81
Covid-19, 4, 1
CPD, 91

D

Daniel Priestley, 75
David Bandler, 95
Depression, 1
Doctor, 1, 22

F

Food, 16, 17

H

Habits, 7, 73, 74, 75
Hitler, 15
Hypnosis, 97

I

Inner Child, 7, 46
Inputs, 6, 11

K

Key Person of Influence, 75

L

Lovable, 32, 37, 42
Lucia Capacchione, 46

M

Marisa Peer, 3, 4, 30, 42, 62, 95
Martin Luther King, 15
Mind, 6, 8, 9, 11, 27

N

Nature, 6, 23, 37
Neuroscience, 6, 23, 27
NLP, 2, 95
Nurture, 6, 23, 25, 26, 37

P

Parents, 6, 25, 27
Pictures, 49, 57
Power, 6, 9, 74
Program, 66, 67
Purpose, 7, 49

R

Rapid Transformational Therapy, 4, 95
Reframe, 6, 36
Repel, 87, 90
Repetition, 16, 75
Roger Bannister, 58
Root Cause, 6, 22, 30, 31

Routine, 74, 76
RTT, 4, 5, 37, 42, 46, 62, 94

S

Simon Sinek, 52
Speigle, 4, 77, 78
Styles, 7, 84
Subconscious, 6, 9

T

Talking Therapy, 1, 2, 30
Therapist, 3, 5, 37, 42
Therapy, 4, 30, 62, 94

U

Upgrade, 7, 42, 48, 49

W

Winston Churchill, 14
Words, 13, 14, 49, 59, 65

Y

You Tube, 60

Printed in Great Britain
by Amazon